On Being Black & Healthy

HOW BLACK AMERICANS CAN LEAD LONGER AND HEALTHIER LIVES

GEORGE BERKLEY

A SPECTRUM BOOK

Prentice-Hall, Inc., Englewood Cliffs, N.J. 07632

Library of Congress Cataloging in Publication Data

Berkley, George E.
  On being black & healthy.

  "A Spectrum Book."
  Bibliography: p.
  Includes index.
  1. Afro-Americans—Health and hygiene.   2. Afro
  –Americans—Diseases.   3. Afro-Americans—Nutrition.
  I. Title.   II. Title: On being black and healthy.
  RA448.5.N4B37   613′.08996073   81–15817
                                              AACR2

ISBN 0-13-634394-5

ISBN 0-13-634386-4 {PBK.}

Editorial production/supervision and interior design
by *Heath Lynn Silberfeld*
Manufacturing buyer: *Cathie Lenard*

This Spectrum Book is available to businesses and organizations
at a special discount when ordered in large quantities. For
information, contact Prentice-Hall, Inc., General Book Marketing,
Special Sales Division, Englewood Cliffs, N.J. 07632.

A SPECTRUM BOOK

10 9 8 7 6 5 4 3 2 1

Printed in the United States of America.

Prentice-Hall International, Inc., *London*
Prentice-Hall of Australia Pty. Limited, *Sydney*
Prentice-Hall of Canada, Ltd., *Toronto*
Prentice-Hall of India Private Limited, *New Delhi*
Prentice-Hall of Japan, Inc., *Tokyo*
Prentice-Hall of Southeast Asia Pte. Ltd., *Singapore*
Whitehall Books Limited, *Wellington, New Zealand*

To my black colleagues,
Herman Hemingway, Quaco Clouterbuck, and Clarence Dilday,
who unanimously encouraged and urged me
to write this book.

Contents

Foreword

Not too long ago professor George Berkley, a white friend and colleague, approached me with an idea he had. He wanted to write a health book for black Americans and wondered what I thought of such a project. Knowing of his interest in the subject of health generally and of his previous work in the field (he has already written, among other things, a fine book on cancer), I urged him to go ahead. I am certainly glad I did for he has produced a book which can benefit all people who are concerned with this most important issue.

      Why do blacks suffer almost twice the rate of high blood pressure as whites? Why is our cancer death rate rising so much faster than the cancer death rate for whites? At the same time, why are we apparently more susceptible to some cancers but less susceptible to certain others? Why does sickle-cell anemia strike so many blacks but almost no whites? Any why during the past twenty years have blacks fallen farther behind whites in most indices of health while their access to medical care during this period has greatly increased?

These are some of the many questions which Professor Berkley has sought to spotlight in this provocative book. They are, to be sure, controversial questions and not everyone will agree with everything the author says. But what he does say warrants careful consideration. I myself urged him to leave in his chapter on hypoglycemia (low blood sugar) when he was thinking of taking it out. My reason for doing so was that the subject, though highly contentious, needed the thought-provoking attention he had given it.

As a black professional trained in the life sciences—I formerly taught chemistry at the college level—I am glad to recommend Dr. Berkley's book. It offers many valuable hints on how black Americans can lead longer and healthier lives. It also should arouse more attention, and stimulate more discussion, on the subject of black health generally. It is a valuable contribution to an important but, up to now, sorely neglected field.

Clarence Dilday, M.S., J.D.

CHAPTER ONE

Black Health: Crisis and Crossroads

I

The 1960s and 1970s saw an explosion of effort ostensibly designed, among other things, to improve conditions for black Americans. Much of this activity failed to match the rhetoric that so frequently accompanied it. Gaps between what was promised and what was delivered were far from rare and, in many cases, far from small. Nevertheless, numerous bills were passed, agencies and subagencies were set up, and programs and projects were launched, all of them aimed, if not primarily then secondarily, at bettering the life and lot of Black America.

These efforts extended into the sphere of health: Medicare and, especially, Medicaid made modern medical care available to millions of American blacks who hitherto, by and large, had had to make do without it. Expanded school lunch programs, along with school breakfast programs in certain areas, also benefited blacks. The nation's burgeoning food stamp program was also thought to help.

Of course, few of these innovations were exclusively or even largely focused on fostering black health. Rather, they were targeted toward improving health care for the poor. However, a disproportionate number of blacks fell into this category and, therefore, found themselves eligible for the benefits involved. By 1977, the average black was seeing the doctor 4.6 times a year. This almost equalled the number of visits made by whites (5.0) and surpassed the number registered by Hispanics (4.2).

What effect did the increased availability of medical care have on black health? From 1950 to 1970, the age-adjusted death rate for black males dropped 4 percent while for black females it went down a full 26 percent. This seems to be a rather remarkable achievement until we remember that the death rate for whites went down as well. For white females it went down 22 percent, a substantial decrease, though one that failed to match that registered by black women. Thus, as far as females were concerned, some narrowing of the mortality gap was achieved. However, the black male death rate dropped only about one-half as much as the white rate. All in all, a sizable gulf remained between the two races with the black mortality rate in 1970 running some 50 percent greater than the rate for whites (10.4 to 6.8).

From 1970 to 1977, the overall gap does seem to have narrowed slightly, for while the death rates for both races continued to fall, they fell a bit more for blacks of both sexes than for whites (down annually 2.9 percent for black females versus 2.3 percent for white females; down 2.2 percent for black males compared to 1.9 percent for white males). However, a more detailed look at the problem shows that even this slight relative gain rests on rather shaky ground.

Turning first to infant mortality, we find in Table 1 that it dropped from 43.9 per 100,000 blacks in 1950 to 23.6 in 1977. This was indeed a substantial and most welcome development. But infant mortality for whites during the same

TABLE 1
Infant Mortality Trends

Group	Deaths per 100,000	
	1950	1977
Black	43.9	23.6
White	26.8	12.3
American Indian	82.1	15.6
Japanese	19.1	6.6
Chinese	19.3	5.9

Source: *Health, United States 1979*. Department of Health and Human Services, 1980.

period went from 26.8 to 12.3. This means that while the number of black infants surviving to their first birthday had, for each 100,000 born, increased in terms of absolute numbers, the black infant survival rate *as a percentage of the white infant survival rate* had actually gone down! To put it another way, the figures show that in 1950 the proportion of black infants dying before their first birthdays was 64 percent higher than for whites; by 1977 the black rate was nearly double that for whites. Thus, the Department of Health and Human Services could conclude, in a report issued in 1980, that "the gap between white and black infant mortality rates had actually increased during the past 27 years."[1]

---

[1]Infant mortality rates for American Indians and Chinese Americans show still sharper drops than those achieved by whites, let alone blacks. In 1950, infant mortality among American Indians was running at 82.1 or almost double the rate for blacks. By 1980 it had nosedived to 15.6 or only about two-thirds of the black rate. The Chinese-American infant death rate was 19.3 in 1950 or about 72 percent of the white rate that year and was only 5.9 in 1977 or less than one-half the death rate for white infants during the year.

If the differences in infant death rates fail to explain the slight relative gain made by blacks over whites in mortality from 1950 to 1977, then we must turn to the adult mortality tables for the answer. Here, however, we find figures that not only fail to reveal any real reason for the relative gain but, on the contrary, point to a relative loss instead.

To start, blacks did manage to gain a sliver of ground on whites when it came to the country's number-one killer, cardiovascular (heart) disease. As Table 2 makes clear, such disorders took, proportionately, 39 percent more black lives than white in 1950 and 37 percent more in 1977. This was hardly a gain yet it does represent some shrinkage in the death rate differential, and given the prevalence of such disorders,

TABLE 2

Ratio of Black Deaths to White Deaths

Each figure below represents the number of blacks per 100,000 who die from the stipulated cause for every white dying from the same cause.

Cause of Death	1950	1977
Cardiovascular Disease	1.39	1.37
Cancer	1.04	1.31
Lung	.80	1.32
Digestive	1.05	1.44
Diabetes Mellitus	1.24	2.21
Accidents	1.28	1.27
Suicides	.36	.54
Homicides	11.73	6.58

Source: *Health, United States 1979.* Department of Health and Human Services, 1980.

such a decline makes itself felt in the overall mortality figures.

But when we look at the nation's number-two killer, cancer, we find a fearful reverse trend afoot. In 1950 the black cancer death rate was 4 percent higher than the white rate. In 1977 *it was 31 percent higher.* The increase was particularly marked in lung cancer, for in 1950 the black death rate came to only 80 percent of the white rate while in 1977 it was 32 percent higher than the white one. The relative increase in cancer deaths was also quite strong for cancers of the digestive track which, after lung cancer, form the second most lethal group of malignancies. Here the black-to-white death ratios rose from 1.05 in 1950 to 1.44 in 1970. In other words, for every 100 whites who died from such cancers in 1950, some 105 blacks lost their lives. In 1970, for every 100 white deaths from this form of malignancy, there were 144 black deaths.[2]

When we shift our attention to the nation's third greatest taker of adult life, diabetes, the relative rise in the black death rate becomes more startling still. While "only" 24 percent more adult blacks than whites died of diabetes in 1950, by 1977 this disease was snuffing out 121 percent more black lives than white lives.

Three other major causes of death are on the Department of Health and Human Services list: accidents, suicides, and homicides.

As Table 2 shows, the black/white ratio for accidental deaths remained about the same during this 27-year period. Not so, however, for suicide. This was the only cause of death for which blacks experienced a more favorable rate than did whites in 1950. The proportion of blacks taking their own lives came just slightly more than one-third than for whites that year. In 1977, the black suicide rate was still running

---

[2]These rates are adjusted to account for population differences.

below the white rate but to a much lesser degree. The black-to-white suicide ratio was now .54. So once again we find that, relatively speaking, ground had been lost, not gained.

Finally there is homicide, and it is here that we find a very substantial *relative* reduction. In 1950, a black person was almost twelve times more likely to lose his/her life through homicide than a white person. By 1970, blacks were a little more than 6½ times more apt to become homicide victims.

This relative reduction, however, does not mean that safety for black Americans actually increased. On the contrary, the number of blacks falling victim to homicide actually went up more than 25 percent. But for whites the relative rise was even greater, with the number of white homicide victims per 100,000 population more than doubling.[3]

Our investigation of relative death rates indicates, therefore, that the slight progress made in narrowing the differential between white and black mortality was achieved only through an increase in the number of white homicide victims. Without this increase, the gap between the two races would not only have remained as large as it was before the programs of the 1960s and 1970s but would have actually widened. Of course, black health in many areas did improve, but in most instances, as we have seen, the improvement was less than that experienced by whites.

When we look at indices other than death rates, we find equivalent evidence showing that greatly increased access to medical care in the 1960s and 1970s did not necessarily abolish or even abridge the racial health gap. In

---

[3]The actual figures were 2.6 in 1950 and 5.9 in 1977. It is interesting to note that not only was the rise in the number of black homicide victims relatively less but that it did not follow a straight line. Thus, while the black homicide rate was 30.5 per 100,000 in 1950, it rose to 51.5 in 1972 before falling to 38.8 in 1977. No ready explanation exists to explain the decrease since 1972, although an improvement in emergency care in major metropolitan hospitals possibly kept many black assault victims from becoming homicide victims.

1977 blacks, on the average, spent almost 20 percent more time in the hospital and over 30 percent more days in bed than whites. What's more, when asked to assess their own health, 11 percent of a sample of whites rated their health as poor or only fair while over 19 percent of a sample of blacks gave their health such an inferior rating.

The conclusion from all these facts and figures is all too obvious. The state of health of Black America is far from good. After two decades of greatly increased access to the medical system, the health gap separating blacks from whites actually appears to have grown. Only a substantial rise in the number of white homicide victims has prevented the differential in death rates between the two races from actually widening.

Why is this so? Why hasn't an increase in the amount of medical care available for blacks relative to that available for whites failed to produce an increase in black health relative to that of whites? Could blacks by nature be physically or physiologically inferior?

The answer to the last question is obviously "nonsense!" Indeed, the data, if it suggests any genetic differences at all between the races regarding health, would tend to support just the opposite conclusion. While blacks have tended to succumb more easily than whites to certain ailments prevalent in modern society, they have, at the same time, produced more than their share of exceptionally long-lived people. The longest-lived American on record is former slave Charlie Smith, who died in 1979 at the reputed age of 137. He may not actually have lived that long, but a geriatric physician who examined him in 1978 came away convinced that Smith had "survived an incredible number of years," and the Social Security Administration acknowledged him as the nation's oldest living person.

Early in 1980, a Senate committee invited a group of able-bodied and sound-minded people who were over one-hundred years old to testify at a hearing. Nearly one-third of the group were blacks. A few months earlier the Associated Press did a story on five exceptionally old and exceptionally spry and alert Americans. Two of the five were former slaves.

More substantial than this anecdotal evidence is the evidence available from Africa. There, blacks have frequently demonstrated remarkably favorable patterns of health despite unfavorable climatic and other environmental conditions. And just as white artists such as Picasso drew on African sculpture for their "new" developments in art and white musicians went to black musical forms for new ideas and inspiration, so in recent years have many white health specialists started to study and learn from African health practices. In the pages that follow we will frequently draw on what they have learned.[4]

But if genetics or inherent racial traits do not explain why black health in America has not improved but, on the contrary, has actually worsened relative to white health during the past few decades, we must look elsewhere for answers. We may find them in the character of the current American lifestyle and the current American medical system.

II

From the standpoint of health, the contemporary American lifestyle affords numerous advantages over previous practices in older societies. Refrigeration, for example, has been a boon in preventing rottenness and rancidity of foods, a problem which has plagued people all over the world from the be-

---

[4]A Portuguese/American chemist who spent some time in Angola when that country was still a colony of Portugal tells me that many white settlers very much preferred native doctors to the white doctors they had brought with them from home. Native remedies, so he said, proved far more effective than European ones for many ailments.

ginning of man's existence. Many noxious and deadly molds and fungi which frequently infected plants and many of the diseases which so often struck lifestock have also been subdued, if not altogether snuffed out. Sanitation practices have improved immeasurably with an attendant improvement in environmental health. For example, diphtheria, which took the lives of so many children in the previous century, resulted to a great extent from the horses who dumped millions of tons of manure and gallons of urine on American streets daily. Many people don't realize it, but the automobile has eliminated much more pollution than it has created.

Despite all these advantages and advances, modern living, when it comes to health, has also produced some new perils. New methods of growing, processing, and preparing food have created health hazards of their own. Many other aspects of modern life have done the same. These new problems affect Americans of all races and backgrounds, but they appear to affect blacks somewhat more than whites. The reason may be that the modern American lifestyle is simply more alien to black experience and heritage. Those from European backgrounds may, from longer experience, have become better outfitted to handle it than those whose fore-bears came from Africa. This point will be extensively explored as we examine specific ailments which seem to strike blacks more severely than whites, though they certainly leave neither race unscathed.

The second reason for the failure of relative gains in health care to produce commensurate gains in relative health lies in the nature of the health-care system. It is not, strictly speaking, a health-care system at all. Rather it is a medical system geared almost entirely to curing illness, not preventing it.

Of course, curing illness bears a distinct relationship to fostering health. It is certainly hard to be healthy when you are sick. But the relationship is not as clearcut as one might at first glance suppose. Sometimes what appears to be the most expedient way of curing or at least alleviating illness only creates the possibility of even greater illness, either in another area of the body or at another time. Furthermore, and this is most important, a health-care system focused on curing illness must have illness in order to function. Without illness there is no work for it to do. If you stop and think about it, you will realize that if the health-care system successfully promoted health, virtually all its practitioners and institutions would go bankrupt!

As a consequence of this peculiar and actually perverse system, the typical American doctor knows remarkably little about the factors and forces which foster health. As a matter of fact, the typical physician is not especially healthy himself. When compared with equals in terms of education, intelligence, and age, our doctors actually tend to get sicker sooner and to die younger.

One way in which the ignorance in matters of health of most, though fortunately not all, physicians shows itself is in their approach to nutrition. Always a vital part of any system for building health, it has become still more important in recent years thanks to a veritable explosion of exciting research activity. Yet, the average physician knows very little about this research, for while most of it has been published in various scientific journals, it has not appeared in the very few medical journals that physicians read.

To take a very specific example, a good deal of new and highly valuable information has come to light in recent years regarding the key role which certain trace minerals play in human health. Much of this research has emanated from the Trace Mineral Laboratory at Dartmouth Medical School, although many other reputable medical–scientific institutions have also contributed to this potentially rewarding field of scientific investigation. Though most of these discoveries have been reported in reputable scientific periodicals, few of them have appeared in medical journals. So the chances are that your own doctor knows next to nothing about them. Indeed, the chances are that your doctor doesn't even know that Dartmouth Medical School has a trace mineral laboratory!

Even when it comes to more mundane aspects of nutrition, the average American doctor fails to pass muster. In 1979 a popular tabloid weekly (*National Inquirer*) asked a Professor of Nutrition at Cornell University to devise a test of ten questions covering basic nutritional lore. The professor was happy to do so. One of the questions he devised was "How much iron does the average woman need in her daily diet?" Another question asked of the physician examinees was "What items contain the most and the least number of calories?" on a list of common foods. A third question asked the physicians to pick the six items with the most salt from a list of ten foods.

The newspaper gave the test to 120 doctors attending a seminar conducted by the American Medical Association. The results? Not one of the 120 answered all the questions correctly. Two answered nine correctly, while two others answered only eight and eight more answered only seven correctly. This means that *108 or 90 percent of these physicians completely flunked this test.*

If you are still not convinced of this point, you may be interested in what happened when a nutrition test was administered at Harvard Medical School. It was found that the average physician teaching at the school knew just a bit more about nutrition than the average secretary at the school. This, at least, was the case when the secretary was not overweight. The average overweight secretary, so it seems, knew just a bit more about nutrition than the average doctor at this, the nation's most prestigious, medical school!

Even when physicians do demonstrate an interest in and a concern for proper nutritional practices, their inattention to developing research in this area, coupled perhaps with an understandable desire to conform to established dogmas, frequently causes them to espouse disproved or outmoded theories. The controversy concerning eggs and cholesterol provides a vivid illustration of this.

Early investigators of heart disease discerned, or thought they discerned, a relationship between heart problems and high amounts of a fat-like substance in the blood called cholesterol. Those who had suffered heart attacks appeared to have had more frequently a high cholesterol count than those who had remained free of such ailments. A connection between high blood cholesterol and a disposition to heart problems seemed clear.

From this fact they reasoned that eggs, which contain a lot of cholesterol, would cause, or at least create a suscep-tibility to, heart attacks and related ailments. So began a campaign aimed at persuading Americans to eat fewer eggs. The campaign proved quite successful, at least in meeting its immediate goal, for egg consumption steadily declined. In 1960, the average American consumed about seven eggs a week. By 1970, this number declined to six, and by 1980 it was down to approximately five. Thus, better than a 25 percent drop in egg eating occurred over the span of twenty years.

But while Americans were avoiding eggs, research was proving that eating eggs would not increase the choles-terol count in anyone with normal metabolism. Only those few individuals who had difficulty absorbing and assimilating eggs had to worry. The rest of us, so study after study confirmed, could pretty much eat two or even more eggs a day with relative impunity.

Far from threatening us by creating cholesterol prob-lems, eggs, so some additional research has strongly sug-gested, may actually help protect us from heart problems. One study, conducted by two research physicians as part of a larger study they were doing for the American Cancer

Society, found that of a group of more than 800,000 followed for six years, those who ate five or more eggs a week suffered far *fewer* heart attacks than those who ate less than five eggs weekly. Another piece of evidence came from a program adopted by the Boston Police Department. Some 400 overweight and largely middle-aged policemen were placed by the consulting physician on a weight-reducing diet. As part of this diet, they were to eat several eggs daily. A follow-up study done eight years later found that *not one of these egg-eating policemen had suffered a heart attack.*

The myth of eggs endangering the heart continued to haunt American "health care" until the spring of 1980 when the Food and Nutrition Board of the National Academy of Science finally shot it down. The Board unanimously found the belief to be without any scientific basis. Even so, many cardiologists continued to cling to the now discredited dogmas about eggs.[5]

What about black health-care practitioners? Do they share this apparent aversion to nutrition and other less sophisticated approaches to health care? Or do they put more stress on preventing and less on curing than do their white colleagues?

There are some indications that this is the case. Black medical schools such as Howard, Meharry, and Morehouse do seem to show more interest in programs of public health. Black physicians often seem similarly disposed. Thus, in an article in *Ebony,* Dr. Therman E. Evans, a pediatrician who also serves as Chairman of the Board of Education for the District of Columbia, has written, "We cannot continue to disregard what we eat as if our diet has no effect on our health status. In fact, what we eat is both directly and indirectly related to every major illness we know of . . ."

[5]One minor aspect of the fears about eggs does, however, lay claim to some credence. The dried egg yolks sometimes found in pastries and other processed foods can raise blood cholesterol, for in this form egg cholesterol is difficult for even people with normal metabolism to process properly.

Although many black doctors, nurses, and therapists of various kinds do show more interest in prevention-oriented approaches, they nevertheless remain professionally and financially locked into the nation's overall health-care system and subject to its proscribed procedures and its peculiar, perverse reward system.

Because the "health-care" system is essentially a medical system geared to treating specific ailments and not to preventing such ailments or fostering good health generally, and because people of African descent living in the United States today seem to show increased susceptibility to certain maladies (just as people of European descent living in Africa show increased susceptibility to certain illness), this book has been written. It takes as its starting point the thesis of Dr. Evans, the aforementioned Washington, D.C., pediatrician and school-board chairman: "At the individual or consumer level, each of us must begin to accept more responsibility for our own health."

Dr. Evans does not mean, of course, that one should stop going to the doctor. He merely wants people to realize that good health is largely a matter of individual responsibility and that no one can sit back and rely solely on others to provide it. In like fashion, this book is not designed to discourage you from seeing your physician or from otherwise making use of the care which the country's medical systems supplies. But it does offer some information, along with some suggestions based upon it, for allowing you to cooperate with your doctor and other health-care professionals to ward off or curb the severity of various ailments while building better overall health.

It was with this purpose that it was written and it is with this purpose that it should be read.

CHAPTER TWO

The Number-One Killer

I

High blood pressure is without question the number-one killer of American blacks. It strikes blacks almost twice as often as it does whites, although the latter are hardly immune from its impact. Furthermore, while high blood pressure, or hypertension, affects many more white men than white women, in blacks it shows no such tendency. As a matter of fact, a slightly higher percentage of black women suffer from hypertension than do black men. One more noteworthy observation: Blacks almost everywhere in Africa enjoy lower blood pressure than do whites who live in Africa!

Here are the figures: Approximately 29 percent of all adult black females and nearly 28 percent of all adult black males can be classified as hypertensive. However, an additional 16 percent of all black adults are "borderline hypertensives." In other words, nearly 45 percent of all adult blacks have a blood pressure problem. And, as we shall soon see, over 90 percent of all adult blacks can benefit by lowering their blood pressure.

First, let us make sure we understand just what blood pressure is and how it is measured.

II

The heart functions essentially as a pump. Its main job is to circulate the blood throughout our bodies, allow it to receive fresh oxygen from the lungs, and send that blood through the blood vessels again. It's quite a lot of work, especially when you consider that it must perform this task anywhere from fifty to one hundred or more times per minute. Yet our hearts are normally so well set up that they can carry on this continuous pumping action for one hundred years or more. One crucial criterion in determining whether a heart will last this long is how hard it has to work, and this work effort represents blood pressure. The more force a heart has to exert to pump the needed blood through the body, the greater the likelihood that it will start to break down or cause other problems.

Blood pressure measurements are usually expressed in two sets of numbers, for example, 140 over 90, or 120 over 80. The top and invariably larger figure signifies the thrust of the heart when it is actually beating; the bottom and smaller figure stands for the pressure the heart exerts between beats when it is at rest. The top figure, the systolic, is the one most people use to describe their blood pressure with only one figure. However, both measurements are important, and they almost inevitably go up and down together, although they are certainly not tied together in a fixed ratio.

One often overlooked point regarding blood pressure readings is that they can vary considerably in any single individual depending on time and circumstance. Some people will register a high reading one day and a normal one the next. There is even something called "white-coat hypertension," which refers to the tension some people experience when they find themselves confronting a clinically dressed medical practitioner. As a result, their blood pressure goes up a few notches. To guard against such factors, physicians frequently have blood pressure readings taken on more than one occasion before they diagnose a patient as hypertensive.

Blood pressure takes its toll principally through heart and cardiovascular ailments. Continual overexertion frequently causes the heart to enlarge, and the extra thrust necessary to push the blood through the blood vessels frequently causes these fragile passageways to become distended. But high blood pressure can work its harmful effects in other ways, too. It may cause kidney problems, eye problems, and possibly even cancer.[1]

But now the question arises as to what constitutes normal blood pressure. Some doctors might consider a blood pressure of, say, 148/98 as normal. Others would call it "borderline," while others would consider it to be definitely high. Almost all physicians agree that when a person's systolic blood pressure ventures beyond the 140 mark and when the diastolic reading starts to crowd 100, caution is warranted.

What, you may now be wondering, demarcates the boundary of normalcy on the low side? Here we come to one of the most intriguing and important aspects of the subject. It is extremely rare to find people with chronically low blood pressure. Such a condition does occur, but usually only to rather exceptional individuals, and for them it is usually only temporary. As long as your diastolic reading does not sink below 90, your physician is not likely to become alarmed. On the contrary, he may congratulate you because, within limits.

---

[1] No evidence has ever emerged linking cancer *directly* with hypertension, but a study of some 1500 men conducted by Northwestern University from 1958 to 1972 turned up the interesting, if rather appalling, fact that the men with high blood pressure had a cancer rate that was three times that of those whose blood pressure was judged normal.

the lower your blood pressure, the longer you are likely to live.

Insurance company statistics have long established the link between blood pressure and mortality. A 35-year-old male with a blood pressure reading of 120/80 can expect to live 9 years longer than one whose blood pressure registers 140/95, and 16½ years longer than one whose blood pressure measures 160/100. Does this mean that a reading of 120/80 represents perfection? By no means. These same figures show that lowering your blood pressure to, say, 105/70 will increase your life span even more. Consequently, well over 90 percent of all black Americans could increase their immunity to illness and their expected life spans by lowering their blood pressure.

One cautionary note is needed, however. The above data do not guarantee that you will live longer than any person whose blood pressure is higher than yours or less than another whose blood pressure is lower. Statistics do not work that way. All they can do is provide probabilities, but the probabilities for most black Americans are that lower blood pressure is better, much better.

III

The most important single step that anyone can take to lower their blood pressure, as well as to generally improve their health, is to refrain from smoking cigarettes. Probably no modern-day practice does as much damage to health as lighting up. A pack-a-day smoker has twice as much chance of dying from heart disease as a nonsmoker; a two-pack-a-day smoker's chances are four times as much. In addition, cigarette smoking contributes to, when it does not actually cause, such ailments as cancer—and not just lung cancer—emphysema, and Burger's disease. There is even evidence to suggest that cigarette smoking increases blood sugar levels, thereby aggravating the problems of diabetes.

Cigarette smoking tends to raise blood pressure in a variety of ways. It interferes with the process whereby the blood receives fresh oxygen, thereby forcing the heart to work harder. Once inside the body, cigarette smoke tends to constrict the arteries, and this forces the heart to pump harder to push the blood through narrower and more rigid passageways. Cigarette smoke contains, among other detrimental components, a trace mineral called cadmium, and, as we shall soon see, this mineral constitutes one of modern society's greater health hazards. Finally, cigarette smoking, being addictive to most of those who indulge in it, creates, like any other addiction, a good deal of stress, and stress, as we shall also examine later, tends to boost blood pressure.

With all this in mind it is not difficult to understand why two out of five cigarette smokers die before their sixty-fifth birthday and only a minority of them can expect to see seventy. Really good health is virtually impossible for anyone who smokes and inhales a pack or more a day. Anyone who gives up or refuses to start smoking cigarettes has probably taken the single most important step that can be taken toward achieving a longer and more vigorous life.

For those who already smoke, such a step is more easily dreamed of than done. As most of us who have kicked the habit can testify, it is one of the most difficult things in life for most people to do. However, some techniques exist for helping the smoker get over the hump, so to speak, so let us take a look at some of the most effective ones.[2]

Among the most useful and valuable technique for breaking the cigarette habit is transcendental meditation.

---

[2]The reader who does not smoke may skip to the next section of the chapter, though among the helpful hints for giving up cigarettes, information of interest and use may be found.

Although this term conjures up images of disheveled Indian gurus enveloped in mystical trances, it really involves a simple and practical relaxation technique that confers a veritable bonanza of benefits, of which an easing of the urge to smoke is only one. We will, as a matter of fact, return to it later in this chapter to see what further help it offers in lowering blood pressure. Keep in mind that this method has been tested by responsible scientific researchers, including doctors at the Harvard Medical School, and has been found to be helpful to the human body in a variety of ways. Because of meditation's utility in promoting general health, the accompanying box is included to show the simple steps involved in doing it.

Although transcendental meditation can ease the withdrawal pangs from giving up cigarettes, it cannot in most

---

How to Meditate

1. Choose a quiet relaxed environment with a minimum of noise and other disturbances.

2. Choose a time twice a day when your stomach is relatively empty. In no case should you have eaten during the preceding two hours. Before breakfast and before dinner are probably the best times for meditating.

3. Close your eyes, relax, and think about anything you wish for 30 seconds or so.

4. Then start to say the word "one," or any other meaningless word you may wish to use, to yourself. If, after a while your mind wanders away, as it almost inevitably will, then simply return to repeating the word you have chosen. There may be times when you are so keyed up about something that your mind will wander continually and you will end a meditation session having said your word hardly more than a few times. Don't let that bother you.

5. When you have spent 20 minutes meditating, stop but keep your eyes closed for at least another 2 minutes. Failure to do so can produce irritability and/or headaches.

---

cases erase them completely. The desire to smoke will still make itself felt for some time to come. So here are some additional bits of advice for those planning to chuck cigarettes.

- Increase your physical activity. This can do a great deal to make the transition from smoker to non-smoker less stressful. But make sure that the increased physical activity does *not* take the form of highly competitive sports since these may increase stress.

- Give up the practices you have associated with smoking. If, for example, you are accustomed to sitting down for a cup of coffee and a cigarette, sit down for a cup of tea or a glass of milk or juice instead. If you are used to having a cigarette and a drink when you get home from work, give up the drink for a while or switch to a fruit juice.

- Avoid situations and locations where you are likely to want to smoke. Go to a movie, for instance, instead of a cocktail party.

- Spend as much time as possible outdoors since there seems to be less pressure to smoke in the open air.

- Eat more alkaline foods since research during the past few years indicates that such foods may reduce somewhat your craving for cigarette smoke. Such foods, in descending order of alkalinity, are molasses, lima beans, raisins, dried figs, beet greens, spinach, dandelion greens, brewer's yeast, almonds, carrots, soybean flour, celery, grapefruit, apples, and milk.

- Make sure you get plenty of calcium, magnesium, and B vitamins. All these nutrients affect the nerves and are not only desirable but necessary to successfully handle stress. Health-food stores sell dolomite, which contains both calcium and magnesium. Three or four dolomite tablets a day, plus one or two bone-meal tablets for extra calcium, can appreciably alleviate the stress of withdrawal. B-complex vitamin tablets will also help.

There are several programs available to assist cigarette smokers in surrendering their habits. One of the most successful, and also one of the least publicized, is a five-day program sponsored by the Seventh-Day Adventist Church. Incidentally, Adventist doctors claim to have found a chemical relationship between nicotine and caffeine, thus adding further appeal to the suggestion that giving up coffee while giving up cigarettes may make the whole process easier.

III

Another major cause of high blood pressure, and one that is possibly more pervasive if not quite so pernicious as cigarette smoking, is overeating, the effects of which can be directly and dramatically discerned. The heart must pump blood through the body's blood vessels. The more weight the body has, the more blood vessels it needs to circulate the blood through this extra tissue, and the harder the heart must work to push the blood through the additional passageways. Each added pound of fat requires an additional mile of blood vessels (capillaries) to continually supply it with fresh blood.

With this fact in mind it should come as no surprise that overweight individuals between 20 and 39 years of age have more than twice the rate of hypertension than do those of normal weight and triple the amount of hypertension of those who are below normal weight. It should also come as no surprise to learn that doctors have often scored remarkable success in lowering blood pressure simply by lowering weight. In one experiment conducted in Israel, doctors managed to bring the blood pressure of three-quarters of a group of hypertensive patients down to normal simply by getting them to lose an average of twenty pounds each.

The large link between weight and blood pressure may explain why black women tend to suffer slightly higher hypertension rates than black men. The situation for white men and women is quite different. Approximately 35 percent of all black women between the ages of 20 and 44 are overweight while less than 25 percent of all white women of that age group fall into that category. However, 16 percent of all white men but only 10 percent of all black men who are 20 to 44 years of age are overweight. In other words, black women, on the average, tend to be fatter than white women, while black men, on the average, tend to be thinner than white men. The situation for black women tends to worsen with age, for from 45 to 55 one-half of all black women weigh appreciably more than they should.

Of course, some fat is necessary for both sexes, especially for women. Nature has given the latter an extra layer of fat to protect the unborn baby once the woman gets pregnant. According to gynecologist Dr. Barbara Edelstein, "Females are primarily designed to be baby carriers" and so "this layer of fat remains in place whether they ever become pregnant or not." Consequently, no woman should become frustrated simply because she cannot achieve the slim, lithe figure of a fashion model. Such a figure may not even be healthy. At the same time, this extra layer of fat does need to be kept within bounds since too much weight in either men or women can lead to high blood pressure as well as to many other ailments, including certain forms of cancer. After cigarette smoking, weight control may be the most important thing you can undertake to improve your general health.

Unfortunately, many people find eating almost as addictive as smoking. For such people, losing weight has become a constant battle in which skirmishes may be won but in which the war itself is never successfully concluded. Fortunately, however, some means and methods exist for facilitating the accomplishment of this seemingly formidable feat.

The first thing to do is to give up once and for all the whole idea of crash diets. Such diets are for the most part not only useless but dangerous. Most of the pounds lost in this way are fluids or carbohydrates and not fat. During a crash diet, the body is often deprived of needed nutrients, while simultaneously subjected to a good deal of strain that in itself can elevate blood pressure. (This actually occurs in laboratory animals when they are put on and off crash diets.) And such diets rarely work. A full 95 percent of those who undergo them regain all or most of the weight they lose. There is even evidence that severely restricting food intake triggers something that overstimulates the appetite once the diet is ended. What is needed is a dietary regimen that one can follow throughout life, and the basis for such a food plan, whether overweight is a problem or not, should be *complex carbohydrates*.

You may at first glance wonder about such a suggestion, for carbohydrates are often equated with calories and are therefore considered taboo for someone wishing to shed weight. But this is true only for the simple carbohydrates such as white flour and, especially, sugar. The complex carbohydrates are contained in such foods as whole wheat, rye, and other whole-grain flours; beans of various kinds; and rice, whose white variety is categorized as a complex carbohydrate although the brown variety is much more valuable in this as well as other respects.

Complex carbohydrates, sometimes known as high-fiber foods, help maintain proper weight in two ways. First, they speed the transit of food through the system. This not only helps prevent constipation, hemorrhoids, and other maladies but also keeps many of the calories contained in food from being absorbed. One study shows that only 86 percent of the calories in food containing a certain amount of bran are assimilated into the body while 97 percent of the calories in simple carbohydrates are absorbed.

The second and more important way in which fibrous foods help prevent unnecessary poundage is through giving those who consume them a quicker sense of satiety. This simply means that complex carbohydrates fill you up. An interesting experiment conducted at both the University of Michigan and the University of Southern California graphically illustrates this. A group of students were asked to eat seven slices of whole grain bread each day. Those who did so lost an average of one pound a week, *regardless of whatever else they ate.* Seven slices of whole grain bread, which together contain only about 500 calories, apparently fill a person up so much that a decrease in consumption alone makes a slow and sensible weight loss possible.

Of course no one can or should live on complex carbohydrates alone. Vegetables and fruits especially should be consumed since they not only supply necessary nutrients but also, though to a more limited extent, furnish additional fiber. A large healthy salad eaten *before* the rest of the meal will do a great deal to hold down the number of calories that will be consumed during the remainder of the meal. Meat and fish can also be helpful in losing weight, and so can a small amount of fat, for the latter also tends to give one a filled-up feeling. White flour should be minimized and white sugar completely avoided. Sugar not only fails to provide a filled-up feeling but frequently does just the reverse, that is, it constantly increases the desire for more and more of it. Some people who have studied the subject actually feel sugar is a drug, and they can cite a lot of research to support such a claim.

Other tips on maintaining proper weight suggest that food should be eaten calmly, slowly, and frequently. Beginning with the last, it appears that eating several small meals leads to less weight than packing the same amount of food into fewer but larger meals. The body's capacity to burn calories diminishes as the number of calories poured into it at any one time increases. As Dr. Mark Altshule, a cardiologist attched to Harvard Medical School, puts it, "The number of meals into which the total caloric intake is divided is highly important for the fewer the meals, the greater the likelihood of obesity . . . the patient who has essentially nothing for breakfast and little more for lunch but makes sure to take a large meal with meat and vegetables and dessert in the evening is an excellent candidate for obesity despite what seems to be not an excessive caloric intake."

As for eating slowly, this too tends to control weight in two ways. One is that the eater simply tires of eating before taking in as much food as he/she would have had had he/she bolted down the food. The second and more important factor, however, is that it takes a certain amount of time for our own appetite control mechanisms to work. When the stomach feels full, it flashes a satiety signal to the brain, but it normally takes twenty minutes or so for the brain to receive it. During this interval, the eater tends to go on eating. Eating slowly allows more time for the filled-up feeling to register. And, in connection with this fact, don't be loath to get up from the table while still feeling hungry. The chances are that in a few minutes those hunger pangs will disappear as the satiety signals break through.

The last of the three tips is more controversial. It is based on the belief that food eaten early in the day has a better chance of being burned off than food consumed later. The research on this is somewhat mixed, and the point cannot be regarded as proven. Nevertheless, it makes sense to speculate that breakfast is more likely to get burned up than dinner, and that late-night, before-bed snacks may have the least chance of all. In any case, we know that heart attacks frequently occur late at night after a very large evening meal that taxes the body's food-processing mechanism.

What about exercise? Some note that it takes many, many hours of vigorous exercise simply to burn off the 3,500 calories which represent just one pound of body fat. Is exercise then worth the effort when it comes to losing weight?

It most certainly is. For one thing, viewed over a period of time and as a continuing activity, exercise will pare off poundage. For example, walking an extra mile each day with no additional food intake will result in a 10-pound weight reduction in one year.

But won't that additional mile walk make you want to eat more? It is here that the real role exercise plays in weight reduction comes into play. The additional mile of walking may actually make you want to eat less! Exercise, it seems, enables the "appestat mechanism," the mechanism which controls our appetites, to work effectively. As Dr. Roger Williams, one of the country's outstanding biochemists, has noted, "Lack of exercise has a crippling effect on the appestat mechanisms."

Finally, one should call attention to and even underscore the myriad and mighty psychological factors involved in weight control. Eating for all too many people has become a substitute for affection or a way of babying oneself or a compensation for emotional deprivation of one form or another. Until the eater faces up to this fact, he/she may never fully succeed in maintaining healthy weight. Dr. Joseph Phillips, a psychiatrist at Meharry Medical College put it this way: "The fat is a cover-up for another need, and that need is for good, solid interpersonal relationships. When you have that, there's no need to eat so much . . ."

IV

That salt in some way tends to raise blood pressure is widely acknowledged and accepted. Most physicians now routinely tell their hypertensive patients to cut down their salt intake. And research reveals that people prone to high blood pressure tend, on the average, to consume more salt than others.

Certainly, modern dietary practices make it easy for all of us to take in a lot of salt, for this seasoning is heavily used in food processing. Processed meats, cheeses, cereals, and more are all heavily salted. Pick up a can or package of virtually any food at your local supermarket and look at the label. The ingredients almost always include salt.

Salt is actually a chemical compound called sodium chloride, and it is the sodium in the compound that presents the problem. Sodium is a mineral which the human body needs, but, like so many other useful nutrients, it can become harmful in huge doses. And huge doses of sodium are an unfortunate feature of all too many American diets.

It has been estimated that we need about ½ to 1 gram of sodium each day for good health, and since it takes approximately 28 grams to constitute 1 ounce, you can see that we don't require much salt to get by. According to the National Research Council of the National Academy of Science, most Americans can consume between 3 and 3½ grams per day without causing themselves any great harm, but beyond that amount damage can be done. And the average American, black and white, consumes 4 to 5 grams a day with some "junk-food junkies" taking in as much as 20 grams daily.[3]

---

[3]Another source of sodium is over-the-counter medicines. The usual dose of Alka Seltzer, for example, contains over 1 gram of sodium. Appetite suppressants and nasal decongestants have also been known to boost blood pressure, though the cause here lies not in the sodium but in the other chemicals they contain.

But if the relationship of sodium to blood pressure has become widely known, a new and highly important aspect of that relationship has in recent years come to light, and, sad to say, most doctors at this writing still do not know about it. This concerns the remarkable role of potassium in counteracting the effects of sodium and thereby generally lowering blood pressure.

It is long known that the minerals sodium and potassium are in some way related. For example, in prescribing medicines for high blood pressure, doctors frequently have prescribed potassium supplements as well. Why? Because the medicines they prescribe tend to flush sodium out of the system and to flush out potassium along with it. Since they recognize that potassium is an essential mineral—muscle weakness being the most common sign of a deficiency—they take the precaution of prescribing it.

However, as far back as 1928 medical evidence emerged which showed that potassium could play a positive role in reducing blood pressure. This evidence slowly increased over the years and in the spring of 1978 a substantial study added the final, confirmatory touch. Some researchers revealed the results of an investigation involving nearly 2,000 blacks and whites in three American cities. The study showed that it was not just the amount of sodium a person consumed that influenced blood pressure but *the amount of sodium consumed in proportion to the amount of potassium consumed.* In other words, the ratio of potassium to sodium in a person's diet proved more decisive in determining a person's blood pressure than solely the amount of sodium.

The results of this study have been confirmed by others, including a study involving black and white high-school students in Jackson, Mississippi. At the same time, experimenters have found in experimenting with animals that they can, at least to some degree, offset the blood-pressure-elevating effects of a high-sodium diet by administering extra amounts of potassium in the diet.

Foods That Contain Large Amounts of Sodium and Potassium	
Foods High in Sodium	Foods High in Potassium
Bacon	Molasses
Pretzels	Bananas
Corned beef	Oranges
Frankfurters	Cantaloupe
Ham	Watermelon
Processed cheese	Squash
Margarine	Broccoli
Butter	Tomatoes
Pork sausage	Peaches
Olives	Prunes
Salami, bologna, and other luncheon meats	Raisins

The discovery of the role of potassium in regulating blood pressure casts a still more unfavorable light on the contemporary American diet. Not only are potassium-rich foods (see the accompanying box) relegated to a secondary place on the American dinner table, but modern processing techniques tend to reduce the potassium content of nearly all foods while substantially increasing their sodium content. For example, 3½ ounces (100 grams) of fresh, raw, green peas provide 316 milligrams of potassium and a mere 2 milligrams of sodium. But a similar amount of canned peas contains 236 milligrams of sodium and only 96 of potassium. In other words, the ratios become reversed. Similarly, 1 pound of whole-wheat flour offers nearly 1,700 milligrams of potassium and only 9 of sodium, but 1 pound of Wheaties, actually one of the better breakfast cereals, contains almost 4,700 milligrams of sodium and no potassium at all!

The discovery of the potassium–sodium relationship offers at least a partial explanation for the high susceptibility which American blacks have to high blood pressure. In

Africa, unlike Europe and even Asia, not only are sodium levels low but potassium levels are high. Thus, those of African descent have over the centuries become adapted to a high-potassium–low-sodium diet and may find themselves less equipped to handle the unhealthy high-sodium–low-potassium foods found so frequently today on supermarket shelves. A study of 278 children in Louisiana tends to support such a supposition. It revealed that the kidneys of black children had lower levels of certain enzymes and thus handled sodium and potassium differently. According to the physician who headed up the research project, Dr. A. W. Voors, the black youngsters seemed especially sensitive to sodium.

Fortunately, despite the damaging diets so often consumed by both blacks and whites in the United States, high-potassium–low-sodium foods are readily available. Fruits, especially bananas and oranges, are good potassium sources. So are most vegetables and, to a lesser extent, most unprocessed meats and fish. In the Appendix you will find a table showing the potassium and sodium contents of a wide range of foods.

Also of interest is the belief that smoking may actually aggravate a person's salt-intake problems. According to Dr. Dorothea Lemeh of Meharry Medical College, "Smoking . . . has an adverse effect on the taste buds . . . people who smoke heavily tend to eat highly seasoned foods because they don't taste the food, so they add more salt or may eat foods that are highly seasoned." Dr. Lemeh's findings are another illustration of how poor health practices tend to reinforce each other. Fortunately, good ones tend to do the same.

V

Two other minerals found all too abundantly in modern society can also raise blood pressure. One of these is cadmium, a toxic mineral that is involved in a host of industrial operations. Some of it invariably escapes into the environment where it can cause a great deal of damage to human health. Besides raising blood pressure, it frequently attacks the kidneys.

The connection between cadmium and high blood pressure, as well as its linkage with industrialization, can be seen in the studies done by Dr. Henry Schroeder of the Dartmouth Medical School. Dr. Schroeder found that the kidneys of Japanese persons contain, on the average, about twice as much cadmium as the kidneys of Americans (black and white), while the kidneys of Americans have four times as much cadmium as those of Africans. The rate of hypertension follows the same pattern. It is twice as high in Japan as in the United States and much more common in the United States than in Africa where, until recently at least, it was remarkably rare.[4]

Dr. Schroeder also found that people dying of high blood pressure had more cadmium in their bodies than those dying of other ailments. And he also found that he could immediately produce high blood pressure in laboratory animals by simply adding cadmium to their rations.

The second hypertension-causing mineral is copper. Like sodium, but unlike cadmium, copper in moderate amounts is essential to life. But also like sodium, the amounts being ingested by all too many modern Americans far exceed the small amounts needed for good health. Indeed, copper, says Dr. Carl C. Pfeiffer who has studied it more than any other medical researcher, "is often present in such abundance in our water supply that it has become a *toxic* trace element" [emphasis in the original].

Dr. Pfeiffer believes that copper imbalances suggest

---

[4]A British physician who worked in Kenya in the early 1930s claims that no doctor in the country had ever come across a case of "essential hypertension" in a native Kenyan. He attributed this situation, which contrasts so sharply with the situation regarding blacks in modern America, with the high-potassium–low-sodium ratio in the Kenyan diet.

another reason for the discrepancy in the hypertension rates between blacks and whites. "Blacks have a higher copper level than whites," he notes, "and their hypertension is harder to treat."

As was the case with sodium, however, other minerals fortunately exist to help us combat the deleterious and dangerous effects of cadmium and copper. Zinc, iron, and calcium all tend to neutralize and get rid of cadmium, and zinc tends to flush copper out of the system as well. Dr. Pfeiffer says he has achieved excellent results in giving zinc, along with Vitamin C, to his hypertensive patients who have high copper levels. (And he adds that most of his hypertensive patients do have high copper levels.)

Zinc is found in a variety of foods, but certain seafoods such as oysters and herring are especially rich in this valuable mineral. Liver is probably the best source of iron, but other foods such as kidney beans also have appreciable amounts. (We will go into this more fully when we examine problems of anemia in Chapter Four.) Calcium, of course, is easily obtainable from dairy products, while some kinds of fish are also good sources of this mineral. All these minerals are also available as food supplements obtainable at most health-food stores. Vitamin B_6, according to some research, increases the absorption of zinc in the body.

VI

Aside from whether or not they contain copious amounts of the "good" minerals we have been examining and small amounts of the "bad" ones, some foods do seem to lower blood pressure. At least they have had this effect on many people.

Foremost among such foods is that favorite of folk medicine, garlic. Communications from physicians telling of the beneficial effects they have achieved by having their hypertensive patients eat garlic began appearing in medical journals back in the 1920s. They have continued to appear ever since. A few years ago a British physician described in *Lancet,* perhaps the world's foremost medical magazine, how he had successfully lowered the blood pressure of five patients by having them eat garlic. Shortly afterwards a Greek physician wrote to say that he was not surprised at this since garlic is almost routinely used in his country as an antihypertensive agent.

No one knows just what ingredients in garlic cause it to have this effect. The pungent plant does contain some selenium, a trace mineral that has been the subject of a great deal of exciting research in recent years. It has been definitely established that people living in areas where there is a substantial amount of selenium in the soil have a high blood-pressure rate of only one-third that of persons residing in areas with low-selenium soil. Garlic also contains sulfur, another mineral which may act to curb blood pressure. Or its beneficial effects may come from other unexplained and unknown factors. But the beneficial effects have been experienced by many, and it is to be regretted that this flavorful herb, which aside from its impact on health does so much to enhance the flavor of so many foods, has not been given the place it deserves in black cuisine. In subsequent chapters we will see that garlic's medical benefits extend to many other serious ailments that affect black people.

Vegetables and fruits in general seem to lower blood pressure. Using college students as guinea pigs, medical researchers have been able to raise or lower blood pressure by simply adding or deleting meat from their diets. Another study compared 86 Mormons to 86 Seventh-Day Adventists. Both groups avoid tobacco, alcohol, and other supposed vices. Both groups also consist almost exclusively of white Anglo–Saxons. The only real difference between them is that Mormons eat meat freely while Seventh-Day Adventists discourage meat consumption. The researchers found that while both groups enjoyed below-average blood pressure, the largely vegetarian Adventists could boast of significantly lower blood pressure readings than the Mormons.

Another group of foods which seems to suppress blood pressure is the group we saw earlier which helps so much in weight control. High-fiber foods, so research indicates, can bring down blood pressure in more ways than by simply bringing down weight. This came to light at the end of the 1970s when the *British Medical Journal* reported the results of placing a group of men on a low-fiber diet first and then on a high-fiber diet. The high-fiber diet has an appreciable effect in reducing the blood pressure of those whose readings were high to begin with. Thus, high-fiber foods can improve a person's blood pressure in two different ways. In later chapters we will see that such foods, which play such a predominant role in so many African diets, can produce many other health benefits for African–Americans.

VII

A scientist at the University of Miami once decided to see how some monkeys would react to the noises that human beings must contend with in the course of their everyday lives. He subjected the animals to what in his view represented the sounds encountered by a typical American blue-collar worker during a typical day. He started in the morning with the ring of an alarm clock, then exposed the monkeys to the sounds of a shower, the radio, gargling toilets, and so on through the day. After about 1½ months, the monkeys' blood pressures had climbed nearly 30 percent!

Of course, men are not monkeys, despite the obvious similarities, and hence may not react to everyday stresses quite so dramatically. But some effect is believed, indeed is known, to play a part in pushing up blood pressure.

Undue stress can adversely affect all kinds of people in all kinds of situations. For example, one woman became hypertensive after marrying a rich man whom all her friends considered to be a prize catch. Why? It seems that he kept up three homes, a main one and two vacation retreats. Most people would envy her good fortune in having such facilities at her disposal, but for her the three homes became a nightmare. With domestic help hard to get, she seemed to be spending her life keeping thirty to forty rooms, including a dozen bathrooms, clean. Her blood pressure came down only after she gave up worrying about her three homes and took up some hobbies instead.

But while the rich can suffer from stress, the poor would seem to be its greater victims. And minority groups would logically be the likeliest of all to fall prey to its consequences. Some believe that the discrepancy in high blood-pressure rates between blacks and whites is largely, if not wholly, based on the discrepancy in the amount of stress in their lives. However, while black people obviously suffer more stress than whites do in White America, and while this situation undoubtedly affects their blood pressure, many doubt that it constitutes the crucial component in making blacks so much more prone to hypertension. Discrimination against the Chinese, for example, was at one time very strong, especially in the western United States, where lynchings of Orientals were far from rare. Yet the Chinese have long enjoyed blood pressure averages well below those of American whites.

An interracial study conducted in Michigan a few years ago showed that not only did more blacks have hypertension than whites, but the darker a black person's skin, the more likely he or she was to suffer from such an ailment. Yet the degree of stress does not necessarily correlate with skin darkness, for lighter-skinned blacks frequently find themselves subject to more conflicting pressures than do their darker-skinned brethren. A more likely and logical explanation might be that darker-skinned blacks are of purer African descent and therefore more vulnerable to the problems and perversions that characterize such a large part of the present-day American diet.

Interestingly enough, the same Michigan study showed that darker-skinned whites tended to have *less* hypertension than the lighter-skinned ones. One explanation for this could be that the darker whites included many of those from southern Europe where the consumption of garlic, along with lots of fruits and vegetables, is much higher. To the extent that their descendants still cling to such dietary practices, they may lessen their likelihood of contracting high blood pressure.

Still, emotional stress must be considered a factor in the problem of black hypertension. What can a black person do to deal with it?

The cheapest, easiest, and most readily available device is transcendental meditation, which we have already looked at in a slightly different connection. TM, as it is called, has shown itself helpful in overcoming the cigarette habit as well as in alleviating stress and in lowering blood pressure. A slew of evidence exists to support this finding.[5] Both white and black psychiatrists who have investigated TM have become quite enthusiastic over what it can do to help people cope with the strains and stresses of everyday life. As Dr. Joseph Phillips, a psychiatrist at Meharry Medical College, has said, "TM is definitely an effective method of reducing tension and many of its consequences: migraine headache, insomnia, high blood pressure and the feeling of tension . . ."

Exercise which aids the abandonment of the cigarette habit also helps in a more direct way to lower blood pressure. According to two physicians who studied the subject exhaustively, "Considerable data has accumulated to indicate a modest blood pressure lowering effect of exercise . . ."

[5]For references, consult the bibliographical notes at the end of this book.

Notice, however, that they only attribute a "modest" effect to exercise and in their book they point out that a few studies actually indicate it could do more harm than good. Since exercise is supposed to provide an outlet for tension while simultaneously improving circulation, and since both these measures should appreciably alleviate high blood pressure, why are its effects not more pronounced?

The problem may be that exercise can drain the body of potassium, which can leave it more prone to hypertension. And while it usually also removes sodium from the body, it does so in such a way as to make whatever sodium remains more concentrated and more powerful. Thus the potassium–sodium ratio can be adversely affected through exercise.

A second, and probably more important, effect is the potentially negative stress that exercise can generate when it is competitive. This includes competitive sports as well as solitary jogging, if the jogger insists on pushing to go faster or farther. Research has revealed that such practices can send blood pressure through the roof, at least temporarily.

In summary, exercise can lower blood pressure and bestow a good many other health benefits as well. However, in taking advantage of it, one should (1) maintain a high potassium intake by eating proper foods and (2) choose less competitive forms of exercise, such as swimming, cross-country skiing, or walking. It is not, after all, a mere coincidence that letter carriers live longer than any other occupational group. Dancers also seem to enjoy remarkable longevity, and dancing may well be the most advantageous of the more vigorous forms of physical exertion.

VIII

Turning to other methods for reducing blood pressure, a simple breathing exercise developed by the New York Infirmary has produced truly remarkable results. Reductions in blood-pressure readings have been as high as 33 percent, although drops of 10 to 15 percent are more common. Here is all you have to do:

1. Stand up in a relaxed position.
2. Tense all your muscles as tightly as possibly and count to six, breathing normally all the time.
3. Rest for several seconds.
4. Repeat the exercise 2 more times.

Although you should tense all your muscles, you should not clench your fists or bend any of your joints. And if you find at first that you can't tense all your muscles simultaneously, then start by tensing a group of them, for example, those on one side of the body only. You will most likely be able to tense them all eventually. Finally you should run through the whole exercise procedure *3 times a day*. If you do that, you will most likely start to see your high blood pressure come down within a few weeks. This exercise does not lower blood pressure in people whose blood pressure is already normal.

There are other means and methods of reducing everyday stress. A more organized routine can be a big help. Some people subject themselves to enormous stress just in deciding what they are going to wear for the day. A successful businessman I know has four summer suits and four winter suits and wears them in rotation for a week at a time changing from one group to the other as the season gets colder or warmer. In this manner he has freed himself from a good deal of unnecessary decision making. The use of public transportation can also help motorists, especially those who have to maneuver in rush-hour traffic. People who drive to work on congested roads show higher blood-pressure and pulse-rate readings than do passengers riding on buses, subways, or streetcars, no matter how crowded the public transportation may be.

Finally, strange as it may seem, being honest with yourself and others will help to keep your blood pressure from going too high. Every time people lie or perform almost any act of deception, they subject their physical systems to fairly severe strains. This is why lie-detector tests work as well as they do. Even some of the most accomplished liars have failed to outwit the tests, which means that even they cannot deceive without showing some signs of physical stress. Thus, personal integrity can play an integral part in keeping you healthy.

CHAPTER THREE

Cancer

I

One out of every four Americans will contract cancer, and two out of every three that do will die as a result. This simple, startling statistic has caused some authorities to say that we are experiencing a "cancer epidemic." Certainly, the cancer rate has surged almost steadily upward since the beginning of the century, and, just as certainly, efforts to cope with, let alone conquer, the disease have met with only scattered and scant success.

Breast cancer provides a good, if grim, example of what has happened. The incidence of this illness has steadfastly spiraled since 1930. Indeed, it doubled from 1960 to 1979 alone. Yet the survival rate for those who contracted it in 1979 was not appreciably greater than it was for those who had contracted it fifty years before. As a result, breast cancer has become the single biggest cause of death for American women in the 33- to 55-year age group.

How have blacks fared during the "cancer epidemic?" Are they better off or worse off than whites?

At one time, American blacks enjoyed a lower overall cancer rate than American whites. Going back to 1937, for example, one finds the cancer rates for both black males and black females to be substantially below those for whites in the three most deadly forms of cancer—lung, breast, and colon–rectum. In lung cancer, for instance, the rate for black males was only 60 percent of the rate for white males. Only in uterine and prostate cancer was the rate higher for blacks than for whites, and only in uterine cancer was the difference substantial. In fact, a black woman in 1937 had almost twice as much chance of contracting cancer of the uterus as a white woman, although the black woman was less than half as likely to get ovarian cancer.

By 1969, the situation was well on the way to reversing itself. Blacks, both male and female, were now leading their white counterparts in deaths from cancers of the lung, stomach, pancreas, and esophagus and were closing the gap when it came to cancers of the colon, rectum, bladder, ovary, and breast. By 1977, the colon–rectum cancer rate for blacks, as we saw in Chapter One, had already surpassed that for whites. And by 1978, Dr. LaSalle D. Leffall, Chief of Surgery at Howard University Hospital, could note in an *Ebony* interview that "For no major cancer is the survival rate greater among blacks than among whites. In other words, whites are ahead of us in every major cancer in terms of surviving . . ." It is probably also significant that Dr. Leffall was serving as President of the American Cancer Society that year, the first black ever to serve in this position. His election may signify not only an increased opportunity for blacks to hold positions of leadership in American life but also an increased concern by blacks with the illness which the Cancer Society seeks to combat.

Unpleasant and unpalatable as the statistical trends in black cancer seem to be, there are a few more positive signs and statistics. The mortality rate of cancer of the uterus in black women has dropped drastically since 1939, and though

Breast Self-Examination

Although black women get cancer less often than black men, everyone should be aware of cancer warning signs. For women, this means special attention to the breasts. Breast self-examination (BSE) should be learned and then practiced each month in order to have the best chance to catch any symptoms early, while there is a good chance for successful treatment. If a woman has any signs of breast cancer, such as a breast lump or a change in breast shape, she should see a doctor right away. Most breast lumps are not cancerous, but the only way to make sure is to be examined by a doctor.

Breast self-examination is simple:

1. In a standing position, raise one hand in the air. Use two or three fingers of the other hand to gently explore the opposite breast, feeling for any unusual lump under the skin. Then do the same thing on the other side.

2. In front of a mirror, check both breasts for any puckering, dimpling, scaly skin, or nipple discharge and then lean forward to check for any abnormalities in shape.

3. Finally, repeat the fingertip inspection, this time lying flat on the back with one arm behind the head.

It is important to perform breast self-examination at the same time each month because the breasts change during the menstrual cycle. Menstruating women should perform BSE after the period each month when the breasts are no longer swollen or tender. Women who are going through or have completed menopause should choose the same day each month for BSE.

From *What Black Americans Should Know About Cancer*. U.S. Department of Health, Education and Welfare.

it remains higher than the mortality rate of white women from this particular malignancy, the difference between the two has been appreciably abridged. What has actually happened is that it has dropped for both races thanks to advancements in surgical techniques, and the increased availability to blacks of medical care has caused their once very high death rate from this disease to decline much more than the rate for whites. Here is one instance where more medical care has produced more health. Among black males, testicular cancer continues to be rare, while it has recently shown signs of increasing in whites. And, of course, blacks rarely contract the skin cancers that afflict hundreds of thousands of whites every year, killing about 2 percent of them.

Much more important than these few relative interracial advantages, however, is the growing knowledge of many of the causes of cancer, and with this growing understanding has come the increased possibility for blacks, and whites, to prevent it.

II

Late in 1978 a medical publication asked a number of leading scientific and medical authorities about the steps they personally were taking to protect themselves from cancer. Among those polled was Dr. Arthur C. Upton, who at the time was serving as Director of the National Cancer Institute. As the physician in charge of the federal government's billion-dollar-a-year cancer research facility, Dr. Upton, it would seem, would or should know more about preventing cancer than anyone else. Here is how he described his own cancer-protection program:

> I take vitamin C and a multiple vitamin preparation. I do not drink heavily, although I'll have an occasional drink. I minimize my intake of animal fat. I also take a substantial amount of fiber, including a large amount of green leafy vegetables, and I eat bran for breakfast and try to control my weight. I guess you might say I try to hedge my bets.

The next year shortly before he resigned his position to go on to other endeavors, Dr. Upton slightly but significantly amended his admonition. He now included vegetable fats along with animal fats in his suggested steps for warding off cancer.

As anyone aware of his background might expect, Dr. Upton knew whereof he spoke. A great deal of new information has surfaced in recent years to underscore the role of nutrition in both causing and preventing cancer. Although lung cancer is caused primarily by cigarette smoking, cancers of the breast, colon, rectum, prostate, esophagus, stomach, and bladder may be chiefly caused by improper intake of food and drink. Furthermore, these common cancer killers, as well as others, may at least be inhibited by following Dr. Upton's approach.

Let us start with the first foods he seeks to minimize or avoid—animal and vegetable fats.

The evidence that a high-fat consumption tends to make people more prone to cancer is readily available. One of Dr. Upton's researchers at the National Cancer Institute, Dr. John Berg, has warned that fats, in too great amounts, overstimulate the body's hormonal system. He notes that countries where fat consumption is high have much higher cancer rates.

One country that has drawn the attention of many cancer researchers is Japan. The incidence of most types of cancer in Japan is amazingly low, especially when you consider that it is probably the most polluted country in the world and has quite a modern lifestyle. At one time scientists studying the subject attributed this low cancer rate to genetics. The Japanese, they said, carried inherent, inborn traits that made them cancer resistant. But in looking further into the situation, scientific investigators found that Japanese people who immigrated to the United States and adopted the American diet soon lost this supposedly inherent immunity. While Japanese women living in Japan have only one-sixth the breast-cancer rate of American women, Japanese women in this country suffer nearly the same breast-cancer rate as other American women, or at least they do if they have abandoned their traditional diet.

What is the traditional Japanese diet? It contains very little meat or fats of any kind. Fat makes up only about 10 percent of the calories consumed by the average Japanese, but it constitutes nearly 40 percent of the average American's caloric intake. The Japanese do eat a lot of dried fish, but most forms of fish are fairly low in fat and are richer than meat in many valuable nutrients. Among those nutrients is iodine, which some research indicates plays a decided role in helping prevent breast cancer.[1]

But if too much animal fat can cause cancer, then too much vegetable fat can cause even more cancer. This is especially true if the vegetable fat has been heated or hydrogenated. The latter process involves blowing bubbles of hydrogen into the fat to preserve it from rancidity, thereby giving it a longer shelf life. In one experiment at the University of Nebraska Medical School, one group of laboratory rats was fed heated butter every day while another group was fed heated margarine. None of the rats fed the butter contracted cancer, but *every single one of the rats fed heated margarine came down with malignant tumors.* Margarine is a hydrogenated fat.

Another experiment at Boston University Medical School produced similar results. Researchers took three different groups of rats—one group that had been raised on a low-fat diet, one that had been raised on a diet high in animal fats, and a third that had been fed a diet high in vegetable fats—and inoculated all three groups with a cancer-causing

---

[1]There is one form of cancer in which the Japanese rate substantially excedes the United States rate—cancer of the stomach. It is thought that eating too much smoked and highly salted food may be responsible for this. Icelanders, who also consume a good deal of smoked and salted fish, also suffer from an exceptionally high rate of stomach cancer.

chemical. About 50 percent of those on the low-fat diet contracted malignancies, some 85 percent of those on the high-animal-fat diet so, while 100 percent of all the animals fed large amounts of vegetable fats developed substantial tumors.

Of course, what is true for rats is not always true for humans, but there is evidence to indicate that for vegetable fats this is by all means the case. Many cardiologists have encouraged people to use more vegetable fats in their diets since these fats are unsaturated and as such were believed to reduce the likelihood of coronary problems, as compared to animal fats which are saturated. Follow-up studies show that people who took this advice seriously ended up with an appreciably greater susceptibility to cancer as well as to gallstones. (They also did not gain any additional protection for their hearts, as the 1980 report of the Food and Nutrition Board, cited in Chapter One, pointed out.)

In addition to fats, Dr. Upton's statement also warned against alcohol, at least in amounts greater than an occasional drink. Here, too, a mounting file of evidence exists to bear him out. Dr. Leffall, quoted earlier, believes that drinking causes even more cancer than cigarette smoking. He claims that 30 to 35 percent of all cancers are related directly to cigarette smoking while 35 to 40 percent are derived from alcohol. Cancers of the esophagus and pancreas are among those frequently induced by drinking, and these are among the cancers which are rising so sharply among blacks, especially black males. In 1931, for example, black men had less than four-fifths the death rate of whites for cancer of the esophagus. By 1969, the black male death rate for this cancer was more than three times the white death rate, a direct and dramatic reversal of the 1937 situation.[2]

---

[2]Cancer of the esophagus can, however, have other causes. For example, during the 1970s it was increasing at an epidemic rate in a section of South Africa called the

What about the more positive parts of Dr. Upton's cancer-prevention program? Returning to his statement, you will note that it consists of four components: (1) bran and other high-fiber foods, (2) vegetables, (3) a multivitamin supplement, and (4) an extra amount of Vitamin C. Let us focus briefly on each one in turn.

The role that fibrous foods can play in preventing cancer first came to light at the beginning of the 1970s when one of Great Britain's most distinguished doctors reported on his research in East Africa. Dr. Denis Burkitt found Africans to be almost immune to colon and rectum cancers, which in the United States follow hard on the heels of lung cancer as the greatest cause of cancer death. Why should such malignancies raise such havoc in the health of both black and white Americans while hardly affecting East Africans at all? He studied the situation carefully, and the more he studied it the more he became convinced that dietary fiber provided the answer.

The people he was working with ate a lot of cornmeal and other high-fiber foods, noted Dr. Burkitt. As a result, they generally moved their bowels twice a day, each time evacuating large, and largely odor-free, stools. This was the reason, so he felt, why these people had remained largely free of digestive cancer as well as such other digestive ailments as colitis and diverticulitis. Dr. Burkitt returned to England intent on teaching his countrymen and all others who would listen the lesson which the East Africans had taught him. Thanks to his international reputation—he had achieved fame for having discovered some years before a rare form of

---

Transkei. Its growth was believed to be caused by the lack of an important trace mineral, molybdenum, in the soil and hence in the food supply. In the United States, areas lacking molybdenum frequently suffer from many medical problems, although since no area in the country relies exclusively on its own crops for its food supply, the problems are less severe. Good dietary sources of molybdenum are beans, especially lima beans, kidney beans, and lentils, along with whole grains, especially rye.

cancer—Burkitt gradually began to get his message across. Further research tended to confirm his claims, and so we may chalk up another point for fiber, a substance which, so we have seen previously, can also help in maintaining proper weight and in lowering blood pressure.

Bran is by far the best source of fiber, and it is the source Dr. Burkitt touts and Dr. Upton takes. But many fruits and vegetables, as well as other whole grains, offer additional sources of dietary roughage. Further, most such foods also furnish other weapons for your own personal war against cancer. These include not only valuable vitamins and minerals but some other valuable substances as well.

Research has clearly revealed that certain vegetables harbor factors which inhibit the development of cancer. They include broccoli, cauliflower, cabbage, and Brussels sprouts. According to scientists at the University of Texas System Cancer Center in Houston, this special anticancer ingredient may be chlorophyll. However, a research team at the Veterans Administration Medical Center in New York believes that a group of substances called plant sterols provides the answer. Whatever it is that may enable them to perform this function, many vegetables do seem to strengthen our defenses against cancer and therefore deserve a prominent place in a prevention program.

The role vitamins may play in protecting us from cancer remains somewhat more controversial, yet research is increasingly pointing out their potential benefits. For example, scientists at the Massachusetts Institute of Technology have found that Vitamin A appeared to provide laboratory animals with added protection from certain cancers. Among these were lung and colon–rectum cancers, which, as we have seen, are the number-one and number-two cancer killers among both black and white Americans. In June of 1979, the *Journal of the National Cancer Institute* contained a report indicating a distinct and direct relationship between lung cancer and Vitamin-A intake in humans. Even heavy smokers who consumed relatively large amounts of Vitamin A in their daily diets were able to achieve substantial protection from this virulent form of malignancy.[3]

But the vitamin that has been arousing the most attention when it comes to fighting cancer is Vitamin C. A good deal of controversy has engulfed this issue, but the weight of evidence is increasingly on its side. And the fact that the former director of the National Cancer Institute finds it expedient to take an extra Vitamin-C supplement, beyond that found in the multivitamin supplement he also takes daily, attests to a growing awareness in the medical community of the vitamin's potential for fighting cancer.

Actually, the National Cancer Institute was among the first agencies to establish a link between the vitamin and the inhibition of cancer. A report on research to this effect appeared in the medical journal *Oncology* in 1969. However, this research remained largely ignored by the rest of the medical community, which continued to concentrate on costly curative methods of often questionable effectiveness.

In Scotland, however, it was a different story. There, two physicians decided to try giving what they regarded as huge doses of the vitamin to a group of terminally-ill cancer patients. These patients had already received all that conventional medicine could do for them and were expected to die fairly soon. The doctors began administering 2,500 milligrams of Vitamin C to these people four times a day for a daily total of 10,000 milligrams. The result: *These patients as a group lived more than four times longer than an equivalent group who had not received the vitamin.* As a matter of fact, a few are still alive today, more than a decade later.

The American medical establishment for the most part

---

[3]Carrots, beef, chicken and pork liver, and certain kinds of fish, such as cod, are especially rich in Vitamin A.

showed little interest in this rather remarkable Scottish experiment. As previously noted, medical practice in this country is not nutritionally oriented. Furthermore, doctors are taught in medical school that any vitamin taken in an amount greater than the bare minimum needed to prevent a vitamin-deficiency disease is simply wasted. Many of the country's leading physicians no longer subscribe to this belief, as Dr. Upton's statement well illustrates, yet deep skepticism about the use of vitamins or other nutrients to combat cancer or any other ailment persists. So in the United States the report of the two Scottish physicians remained largely unnoticed and unread.

This was not the case elsewhere, however. In 1977 a Japanese hospital began giving large doses of Vitamin C to its cancer patients. It reported successes similar to, if not exceeding, those recorded in Scotland. Survival rates and life expectancies shot up. Meanwhile, biochemists in the United States continued to report encouraging results in using Vitamin C on test animals. In 1979 Sister Mary Eymard Poydock, a Catholic nun who holds a doctorate in biochemistry and who directs cancer research at Mercyhurst College in Erie, Pennsylvania, published the results of twenty years of painstaking research. Sister/Doctor Poydock had found that a combination of Vitamin C and Vitamin B_{12} would give experimental mice *an almost absolute immunity to cancer.* Given enough of these two vitamins, these animals withstood what would otherwise be lethal doses of cancer-causing chemicals. And giving these vitamins to mice already rendered cancerous greatly lengthened their life spans.

Another research report published in 1979 seemed at the time less favorable to Vitamin C. The world-famed Mayo Clinic had given large amounts of Vitamin C to 150 advanced cancer patients without any appreciable benefit. However, Vitamin C's backers were quick to point out that nearly all these patients had first received chemotherapy or radiation or both, and these techniques usually destroy the immune system.[4] Vitamin C, say its supporters, works only by strengthening this system, and one can no longer strengthen what has already been destroyed.

Those who conducted the experiment acknowledged that the effects of chemotherapy and radiation could have distorted the results. As they put it, "We recognize that earlier immunosuppressive treatment might have obscured any benefit by [vitamin C]."

Thus, Vitamin C has little to offer those who have already contracted cancer and received treatments that have knocked out their immune systems. But for the rest of us, Vitamin C and the other components of Dr. Upton's program provide a solid basis for protecting ourselves from cancer. We should wisely make use of them.

III

Can clams counteract cancer? The question may strike you as pretty preposterous if not absolutely absurd, yet a group of researchers at the AMC Cancer Research Center and Hospital in Denver, Colorado, are not only posing such a question but they are answering it—in the affirmative! Yes, they say, clams, especially the common little neck or cherrystone, appear to offer an antidote to mankind's most dread disease.

Once again we find a nun with a doctorate in biochemistry heading up the investigation. This time it is Sister/Doctor Arline Schmeer who claims to have discovered a substance especially abundant in clams that demonstrates a surprisingly strong ability to counteract cancer. The substance is called mercenene and is found in many kinds of

---

[4]This is the complex physiological system each of us has to combat illness and infection. The white corpuscles of the blood are probably the system's best-known weapon, but it has others as well.

seafood but in clams most of all. Dr. Schmeer and her associates have extracted and purified this mercenene and given it to thousands of mice in which cancer has previously been induced. It has, they say, completely cured the animals 80 to 100 percent of the time. Other researchers, including some at the National Institutes of Health, have confirmed her basic thesis.

The potential use of mercenene as a drug for combating cancer is many years away, for extracting and purifying it is as yet a complicated and costly process. But in the meantime those who wish to avail themselves of its potential should put clams on their list of preferred foods. Even if it doesn't turn out to be of value in helping humans fight cancer, and this is possible, clams contain many other healthful nutrients, including some valuable trace minerals.

Clams are not the only potential cancer fighters that are missing from Dr. Upton's program. There are several other foods which also have shown signs of strengthening the system against malignancy.

One of these is garlic. We have already seen in Chapter Two how this odorous but flavorful herb helps to clear fats from the blood and to lower blood pressure as well, at least in some people. As it so happens, experiments going back to 1957 show that laboratory animals fed garlic resist cancer much more strongly than similar animals raised the same way without having received any garlic. Indeed, in 1977 Japanese scientists actually created an anticancer vaccine from garlic that proved 100 percent effective in protecting test animals from the disease.

These experiments, like so many of the others we have been describing, have been conducted by biochemists who are not allowed to experiment on humans. And since few of those doctors with research grants have shown much disposition to divert their resources into nutritional research, we do not know for sure if garlic or clams will actually help humans resist cancer. However, since what works with test animals in this area often works for people as well, and since garlic even more than clams is a nutritious food in its own right, here is another reason for adding it to your menu.

Garlic is an old favorite of folk medicine. And so is honey. Here again we find some evidence that folklore may have something going for it.

The role that honey may play in preventing cancer first came to light when Russian scientists announced the results of a survey they had done on the country's over-100-years-of-age population. The Soviets had found that an amazing number of these oldsters were, or had been, beekeepers. Since other types of farmers in the USSR do not enjoy any especially long lease on life, they began to speculate that possibly it was the products of the animals they kept that kept them alive for so long. And the best known of these products is honey.

Subsequent studies in other countries showed not only that beekeepers enjoyed long life spans but that they also seemed to demonstrate a remarkable immunity to cancer. A survey conducted jointly by a Vermont physician and the head of the New England Beekeepers Association found only one beekeeper who had had cancer. What's more, this fellow had contracted the disease before he took up beekeeping, and after he entered the trade his cancer cleared up! A more formal study was conducted in France. Investigators there studied the death certificates of one thousand beekeepers. Only one out of the entire thousand had died from cancer.

However, it is easier to demonstrate that beekeepers show a remarkable resistance to cancer than it is to prove that honey is the reason behind such resistance. The bees also produce other products, such as pollen, which is believed to be a greater "health food" than honey. Many athletes have begun taking pollen tablets in recent years, claiming that such tablets give them extra energy. No reliable research has arisen to bear this out, but the coach of the Finnish Olympic team of 1976 attributed his team's surprisingly strong showing over their performance at the 1972 Olympics to pollen tablets. Since beekeepers tend to eat pollen, which the bees bring back from their forays into the fields, as well as honey, it may be the pollen that is providing the protection.

But even if pollen provides some possible health benefit, honey may still have something to offer. First, honey does seem to contain some antiseptic elements. Some athletic trainers claim that it cures athlete's foot, and a British surgeon insists that it makes the best dressing for wounds. Honey, at least in its raw state, also contains pollen, so that whatever healthful ingredients there may be in one may be found in the other. Finally, honey does not disturb our immune systems, as sugar does.

This brings us to another element in the fight against cancer, one that has so far escaped any real notice from most medical authorities—the role of sugar. The consumption of sugar and related sweeteners such as corn syrup has reached enormous proportions in most western countries. The average American ingests well over 100 pounds of such sweeteners each year. Much of the sugar is added to other foods, which are often not thought of as sweetened. For example, most canned vegetables, most canned fruits, and even most "unsweetened" breakfast cereals contain 10 to 20 percent or more sugar. And presweetened cereals sometimes contain more than 50 percent sugar.

Two startling studies were published at the end of the 1970s, indicting sugar as a cause, possibly a major cause, of cancer. The first was a forty-one-country survey conducted in Great Britain and published in the *British Journal of Cancer* in 1979. Refined sugar was found to be the foremost factor in the incidence of breast cancer. More than any other element, dietary or otherwise, consumption of sugar correlated with the likelihood of this form of malignancy.[5]

---

[5]The second most important factor was fat consumption, while protein intake placed third. We have already examined the role of fats in various kinds of cancer. Apparently protein can also be dangerous if consumed too heavily.

A year later the American periodical *Nutrition and Cancer* carried a report showing increased susceptibility to cancer in mice fed diets high in sugar. There appears to be little doubt that sugar, through its effect in weakening the immune system and perhaps other ways as well, should be consumed as little as possible by cancer-conscious people.

Many commonly used drugs have also been suspected, and not without reason, of promoting cancer. A drug called DES (Diethylstilbestrol) was once given to women to prevent miscarriage, but it is no longer administered to humans since it was found to cause cancer in some of the women as well as in some of their children. And the *Journal of the American Medical Association* has said that the "long-term use" of estrogens, which have also been given to menopausal women, is "unequivocally related" to large increases in certain forms of cancer. Blood pressure medicines, especially those containing a substance called reserpine, are also suspect.

One of the latest groups of drugs found to have potential in the promotion of cancer is tranquilizers. A team of British researchers found that administering tranquilizers to cancerous mice caused their tumors to grow much more rapidly. This is of particular concern to Americans who in 1978 purchased 2.5 *billion* tablets of valium, a leading tranquilizer. One study showed that some doctors were almost routinely giving welfare mothers prescriptions for valium to help them through their problem-ridden days, although subsequent studies showed that the more valium one took, the less able one became to cope with problems of any kind.[6]

But if tranquilizers are to be avoided, or at least minimized, then so is the stress which they supposedly seek to alleviate. More and more evidence is pointing to stress as a primary producer of cancer.

---

[6]In July 1980 the Food and Drug Administration issued a warning against the almost routine prescribing of valium and other tranquilizers by many doctors and announced that five drug companies that produce these drugs had agreed to revise their labels to reflect the dangers their continued use may pose.

Cancer Information Service	
Southern California	1–800–242–9066
Colorado	1–800–332–1850
Connecticut	1–800–922–0824
Delaware	1–800–523–3586
District of Columbia (Metro Washington)	1–202–232–2833
Florida	1–800–432–5953
Illinois	1–800–972–0586
Maine	1–800–225–7034
Maryland	1–800–492–1444
Massachusetts	1–800–952–7420
Minnesota	1–800–582–5262
Montana	1–800–525–0231
New Hampshire	1–800–225–7034
New Jersey	1–800–523–3586
New Mexico	1–800–525–0231
New York City	1–212–794–7982
New York State	1–800–462–7255
North Carolina	1–800–672–0943
Pennsylvania	1–800–822–3963
Texas	1–800–392–2040
Washington	1–800–562–2875
Wisconsin	1–800–362–8038
Wyoming	1–800–525–0231
All other States	1–800–638–6694

Actually it is not so much the stress itself, perhaps, which causes cancer as the way the individual copes, or fails to cope, with it. Some persons actually thrive on certain kinds of stress, and for them the absence of such stress would probably be more perilous. Those who are really endangered are those who experience a great deal of stress and lack outlets for their feelings. Those, in other words, who keep their fears and their hates locked up inside them. Study after study shows that such supposedly self-contained people place themselves in much more peril than do those who have found suitable ways to "let off steam." Hospitalized cancer patients who complain a lot tend to do better against their ailment than do those who simply and silently do as they are told. Even those who keep up their spirits and get along well

TABLE 3
What Are the Warning Signs
of the Different Forms of Cancer?

Listed below are the major forms of cancer and the warning signs for each. These symptoms do not mean you have cancer, but if they last more than two weeks you should see a doctor without delay.

Major Forms of Cancer Warning Signs

Lung	Cough that won't go away or long-lasting breathing problem.
Breast	Lump or thickening of the breast. (*See also* the boxed material about breast self-examination.)
Colon and Rectum (Large Intestine)	Changes in bowel habits; bleeding from the rectum; blood in the stool.
Prostate	Difficulty in urinating.
Uterus	Unusual bleeding or discharge from the vagina.
Bladder and Kidney	Difficulty in urinating; blood in the urine.
Lymphatic Organs	Enlarged lymph nodes.
Mouth and Throat	Sore that does not heal; hoarseness; difficulty in swallowing.
Stomach	Indigestion that won't go away.
Blood-forming Organs	Repeated or continual tiredness; tendency to bruise and bleed easily; frequent infection.
Skin	Sore that does not heal; change in a wart or mole.

From *What Black Americans Should Know About Cancer*. U.S. Department of Health, Education and Welfare.

with the hospital staff also seem to fare better than the silent sufferers.

Just why suppressed stress has this effect is not fully known. It is a fact that stress of any kind will increase our need for various minerals and vitamins. As an article in *Essence* states, "When we're under stress our bodies use more of certain nutrients. For example, your body uses a lot more potassium, which controls the activity of your heart muscle and nervous system. You also deplete your body's stores of vitamin C..." The writer then goes on to ask, "What vitamins does your body need most when it's under stress?" The answer is "vitamins A, the B-complex . . . C and E."

To that list of vitamins I would add minerals such as magnesium, calcium, and zinc, as well as potassium, which the article cites. For other means and methods of alleviating stress, one can refer back to Chapter Two, where stress has also been identified as an aggravating if not causative factor in high blood pressure. Indeed, many of the steps a prudent person would take to combat cancer duplicate in large measure those one would take to lower blood pressure. This is yet another indication that good health generally provides the best protection against all manners of disability, disease, and death.

CHAPTER FOUR

Diabetes

I

While cancer has become the most dreaded disease in contemporary America, diabetes takes almost as many lives. Some 300,000 Americans, white and black, die from diabetes every year compared to approximately 360,000 who are killed by cancer. To put it another way, the average diabetic in this country can expect to live only three-quarters as long as the average nondiabetic.

In addition to its effect on longevity, diabetes can and often does produce a host of medical problems. These may include various circulatory dysfunctions affecting organs as seemingly unrelated as the eyes and the feet. Diabetics frequently fall prey to gangrene in the lower extremities as they get older and sometimes require amputations of the feet or the legs. They also become susceptible to cataracts and other eye disorders. About 10 percent of all legally blind Americans are diabetics.

Diabetes is the fastest growing of all the major health

Warning Signals of Diabetes

Juvenile-onset diabetes is characterized by the sudden appearance of:

- Constant urination
- Abnormal thirst
- Unusual hunger
- Rapid loss of weight
- Irritability
- Obvious weakness and fatigue
- Nausea and vomiting

Any one of these signals can mean diabetes. Children usually exhibit dramatic and sudden symptoms and must receive prompt treatment.

Maturity-onset diabetes may include any of the signs of juvenile-onset diabetes or:

- Drowsiness
- Itching
- Family history of diabetes
- Blurred vision
- Excessive weight
- Tingling, numbness, pain in the extremities
- Easy fatigue
- Skin infections and slow healing of cuts and scratches especially on the feet.

Many adults may have diabetes with none of these symptoms, and the disease is often discovered during routine physical examinations.

Source: From *Diabetes: The Number 3 Killer.* American Diabetes Association, 600 Fifth Avenue, New York, NY 10020.

hazards in America today. Already, over 10 million Americans, nearly 5 percent of the population, are believed to suffer from some form of this disease. Random samplings of the population have indicated that a large number of Americans are walking around with this disease and do not know it. The exact figure cannot be pinpointed, and the fact that so many can have diabetes and not know it illustrates that a good deal of difference exists in the effects that the disease has on different individuals.

There are actually two forms of diabetes—juvenile onset and maturity onset (or adult onset). Juvenile onset is the most serious form. As its name suggests, it usually begins fairly early in life and, more often than not, will require insulin treatments. (We will go into this in more detail shortly.) Adult-onset diabetes, also in accordance with its name, strikes later in life and usually is much less severe. Most adult-onset diabetics can cope with their condition through wise management of their diet.

In addition to the 10 million who are believed to be full-fledged diabetics, there are countless millions, and possibly even tens of millions, who experience some degree of difficulty in controlling their blood sugar levels, which is what diabetes is all about. This becomes especially true as people get older. As Dr. Robert Atkins, the nutritionally oriented New York physician who has written extensively on health, puts it, "It is safest for a doctor to assume that *everybody* is in need of blood sugar control."

If, as Dr. Atkins says, it is safe to assume that everybody can use some advice and assistance in controlling their blood sugar, then it apparently is even safer to assume that blacks need such help. As with high blood pressure and with many forms of cancer, so with diabetes: Blacks show substantially more susceptibility to this ailment than do whites.

The figures per 1,000 for known cases of diabetes are:

	Female	Male
Black	35.00	21.8
White	24.30	20.0

The first thing these figures reveal is the far greater susceptibility of black women than black men to this illness.

The diabetic rate for black males is 9 percent greater than that for white males, but the rate for black females is nearly one-half again as high as the rate for their white counterparts. Why this difference?

For Dr. W. Lester Henry, diabetes specialist at Howard University Hospital, the answer lies in the greater predisposition of black women to becoming overweight. "There is no doubt that when people become obese," he says, "they become insulin resistant, and they are, in a sense, digging their graves with their teeth."

The figures do tend to support Dr. Henry's thesis. It will be recalled from Chapter Two that black women experience greater problems with weight control than white women do. And other figures show that 60 to 80 percent of all people who become diabetic first become overweight. Nevertheless, there are grounds for believing that while obesity may explain some or most of black females' increased vulnerability to diabetes, it does not explain it all.

For one thing, the figures show that black males contract diabetes more often than white males, even though the degree of difference in this case is not so large. And in considering the case of black males we must keep two additional factors in mind. First, black men, as a group, go to doctors and monitor their health somewhat less assiduously than white men do. Consequently, there is probably a higher percentage of them in the "diabetic-but-don't-know-it" category. Second, if you recall the figures from Chapter Two, you will remember that while black women were significantly more overweight than white women, the reverse was true for black males. The rate of obesity in black males is nearly 50 percent less than that for white males. Thus, if obesity were the only factor, the black-male rate for diabetes would be substantially lower instead of higher than the rate for white males.

As for the other factors that may be involved, we are

again left with the hypothesis that those of African descent are less physically adaptable to the contemporary American diet than are those whose ancestors came from Europe. There is not, it should be stressed, a shred of what can be called solid scientific evidence to prove conclusively that this is the case, but there are grounds for speculating along this line. For in addition to the indication that obesity does not seem to be the only factor involved, we have two other facts worth noting. One is that we have some evidence about hypertension which indicates that blacks seem to experience greater difficulty than whites in handling the lopsided sodium–potassium ratios that characterize the typical American diet. It therefore does not seem all that strange to wonder whether they might not also experience greater difficulty than whites in handling the enormous amounts of sugar in this diet as well. Historically, blacks have had much less exposure to the refined sugar which today they, along with white Americans, are consuming in such copious amounts.

The second fact which lends some support to this supposition is the experience of other non-European peoples who have suddenly found themselves eating a lot of refined sugar. Almost invariably, such peoples start to develop high rates of diabetes. Yemenite Jews, for example, rarely contract the disease in their ancestral Arab homelands. Once they migrate to Israel and become exposed to its semi-Western diet, their rate of diabetes shoots upward. The same has proven true for Eskimos and American Indians. The Pima Indians of Arizona, for example, now have a diabetes rate of over 30 percent, which is far and away the highest in the world.

In any event, modern medicine, although unfortunately not all of its practitioners, knows a great deal about how to prevent diabetes from developing and how to control it once it has developed. To quote Dr. Atkins again, "If ever there was a condition that something could be done about, it would be diabetes—because diabetes is almost totally nutritional in its causation." Let us now look at some of the nutritional factors, as well as others, that play a part in the prevention and control of this rapidly spreading scourge to black longevity and health.

II

The human body cannot directly assimilate the sugar most of us consume every day. Before its assimilation can take place, this sugar must undergo a process that will convert it into another form. And to carry out this conversion, insulin is necessary.

Insulin is a hormone generated in the pancreas gland, and in most cases this gland can and will produce enough insulin to convert into glucose all the sugar that enters the bloodstream. When its machinery fails to function adequately, problems arise. And when this malfunction continues, another case of diabetes is likely to occur.

The three most common symptoms of this disease are excessive thirst, excessive urination, and excessive fatigue. A sudden or unexplained weight loss can also signal its impending arrival. Once diabetes has struck, it is virtually impossible to fully eradicate it. A diabetic must generally expect to remain a diabetic for the rest of his or her life.

But that does not mean that the diabetic's condition is hopeless. With proper dietary management most, though certainly not all, diabetics can enjoy a normal or near-normal life and can expect a normal or near-normal life span. My own mother is a diabetic approaching 80 years of age and enjoying remarkably good health; my wife's grandmother, also a diabetic, lived vigorously until the age of 86. More importantly, most people, regardless of race or age, can probably avoid diabetes by taking advantage of what relatively recent research in the field has revealed. And given their apparent greater susceptibility to the illness, black Americans would do well to familiarize themselves with, and carefully follow, the practices it suggests.

The first of these concerns cutting down on the ingestion of sugar. This seems natural enough to a layperson who begins to think about the subject, but, oddly enough, it did not become an accepted part of medical care until the 1970s. Until then, it was believed that the inability of the pancreas to produce enough insulin resulted exclusively from a genetic deficiency. Some people were simply unlucky enough to be "naturally" poor insulin producers, and, so it was thought, there was little that they could have done to correct it.

Medicine now knows differently. While it is true that some people are born with poorer-functioning pancreas glands and are therefore inherently more prone to develop diabetes, whether they actually do or do not may depend heavily on their diet. The more sugar we consume, the more insulin our pancreas gland must generate, and the more we force it to fulfill this function, the less able it becomes to do the job properly. Called on too frequently to pump insulin, the pancreas starts to tire and to become what medical investigators call "insulin insensitive."

That eating too much sugar would actually create diabetes in people who otherwise might not be overly prone to develop it was first suggested by some work carried on by the United States Department of Agriculture. The chief of the Department's Carbohydrate Nutrition Laboratory, Dr. Sheldon Reiser, and his associates found that feeding rats refined sugar made them diabetic but feeding them simple starch did not. (They also found that the sugar-fed rats got much fatter than the starch-fed ones even though both groups of animals received the same number of calories.)

They then undertook an experiment with human volunteers. The ten men and nine women who constituted the experimental group were given, alternatively, high-starch and high-sugar diets. It was found that their blood sugar levels rose much higher on the high-sugar diet than on the high-starch diet. The sugar, noted Dr. Reiser, entered the bloodstream too quickly, thereby triggering a spurt of insulin from the pancreas. So far this sounds quite predictable and even normal, *but this is exactly what happens prior to the advent of maturity-onset diabetes.* There is customarily a surge of insulin—hyperinsulinism is the term used—and then diabetes starts to occur.

To Dr. Reiser the experiment confirmed the theory that excessive sugar consumption can cause, not just complicate or catalyze, diabetes. More and more doctors and scientists are agreeing with him. Dr. Morgan B. Raiford, founder of the Atlanta Hospital and Medical Center, says, "People who are excessive sugar eaters during the first 40 years of life are much more prone to develop diabetes. They wear out the pancreas trying to produce insulin. It's just like whipping a tired horse."

It is certainly easy for the average American of any race to fall into this position. As noted earlier, sugar in some form or another is found on nearly every shelf in the supermarket. Ketchup, for instance, actually contains proportionately more sugar than some candies. So do some salad dressings. One nondairy coffee creamer was found by *Consumer Reports* to contain 65 percent sugar. And whiskey, gin, and other alcoholic beverages are essentially sugar in a slightly different but certainly no less harmful form.

It has been estimated that sugar makes up 24 percent or nearly one-quarter of the average American's daily caloric intake. This represents a health hazard for all Americans but one that possibly poses still greater peril to blacks since blacks have had less experience in metabolizing it. Hence, health-conscious blacks will cut their sugar consumption to a minimum.

But what about honey, which in the previous chapter we saw as *possibly* related to health and longevity. Is it now to be condemned as a potential cause of diabetes?

Honey certainly contains sugar, lots of it, but most of this sugar is in a different form than that found in refined white sugar. Much of honey's sugar content does not need to be converted in order to be assimilated, and to the extent that it doesn't, it does not tax the insulin-producing capabilities of the pancreas in quite the same way. This does not mean that honey is automatically safe for diabetics, and it does not mean that nondiabetics can eat as much as they want of it without placing themselves in any danger. But the human body does seem more naturally adapted to the sugar found in honey, and while this sweetener may not actually create health, it certainly does little to harm it, judging from the health records of beekeepers.

One welcome advantage of honey is that relatively small amounts of it will usually satisfy a person's craving for sweetness. As a matter of fact, it is almost impossible to eat too much of it since it has a filling quality that refined sugar woefully seems to lack. For this, if for no other reason, those seeking a taste of sweetness would do better to keep a honey pot rather than a sugar bowl on the dinner table. It should also be noted that there is absolutely no evidence that honey, like sugar, weakens the immune system.

As for artificial sweeteners such as saccharine, these too can be of use in alleviating the desire—it is more often a drive—for sweetness that so many of us have acquired. They are probably not good for us. Massive doses of such sweeteners will cause bladder cancer in *some* laboratory animals, but to the extent that we substitute them for sugar we are almost certain to benefit.

III

Diabetes demonstrates a pattern that we have already observed about high blood pressure and cancer: It afflicts more black Americans than white Americans, yet it rarely strikes black Africans who continue living in their native environments and eating their traditional foods. As we have noted, one of the chief characteristics of the diets of most Africans is the presence of roughage. Can fibrous foods play any part in protecting them from the disease which so severely strikes their fellow blacks in America?

This question was first posed in the scientific community by a British physician, Dr. Hugh R. Trowell, in 1972. Dr. Trowell had spent a good deal of time in Africa and had been struck by the rarity of diabetes among the Africans he treated. He was also impressed, as other British doctors have been, by the high fiber content of the meals they consumed. In an article in the *American Journal of Clinical Nutrition,* he wondered if there might not be a relationship. Might not the high incidence of diabetes found throughout the industrialized world be due, in part, simply to the lack of food fiber?

Four years later, Dr. Trowell, and everyone else who was interested in the question he asked, had the answer. A group of British physicians reported on a test they had conducted using eleven diabetic volunteers. The group was fed their regular diet and then their regular diet with some fiber added in the form of pectin and guar. Sure enough, the additional fiber seemed to have a significant effect on lowering the levels of their blood sugar.

In August 1976, a month after the report of the British physicians was published in the British medical magazine, *Lancet,* a yet more sensational result was reported in this country. Research had been conducted by a medical team from the University of Kentucky College of Medicine in Lexington in association with the Veterans Administration

Hospital in that city, and it was destined to change the whole course of diabetic treatment.

Heretofore, the American Diabetes Association had emphasized a diet consisting of high-protein and moderately high-fat meals, with all carbohydrates kept to a minimum. After all, sugar was a carbohydrate, and if sugar could be disastrous for diabetics, then it seemed obvious that other carbohydrates would prove dangerous for them as well. And since the whole grains, which are the most fiber-laden foods, are carbohydrates, albeit of the complex and not of the simple variety, it stood to reason that they should be given only a marginal role in any diabetic's diet.

In this experiment, thirteen men, some white and some black but all with fairly advanced diabetic conditions, were fed the American Diabetes Association's recommended diet for one week. They were then put on a high-carbohydrate, high-fiber dietary regimen for a period of two weeks. The results were quite spectacular. At the beginning of the experiment all thirteen men were on insulin medication. The Association's diet did nothing to change that. Indeed, most of them had already been following such a diet. But the high-fiber, high-complex-carbohydrate regimen had a remarkable effect. *Nine of the thirteen men improved so much that they no longer needed to take insulin,* while a tenth was able to cut his insulin requirements in half. In other words, over 75 percent of the volunteers responded in a dramatically positive fashion to a diet which up to then the American Diabetes Association had considered dangerous.[1]

Historical investigations have added scope and sub-

---

[1]If you or somebody you know would like to make maximum use of such a diet, ask your physician to write to Dr. James Anderson, head of the experiment, to request a booklet which Dr. Anderson, in association with Beverly Sieling, a registered dietitian, has written. Entitled *HCF Diets: A Professional Guide,* it provides complete instructions on how to develop and place a patient on a high-fiber diet.

stance to these experimental studies. From 1875 to 1895 the United States switched from stone-ground flour to rolled-mill flour. The first method retained most of the natural fiber in the original wheat; the second method produced the pasty white flour used in many of the wheat products Americans consume today. During this twenty-year transformation period, the number of diabetic deaths skyrocketed. Then, during World War II and in the stringent immediate postwar period, Great Britain was forced to use more unprocessed grain for its flour. The death rate from diabetes decreased about 55 percent during that time. By the end of the period, the diabetic death rate for women had reached the lowest level in almost fifty years.

Although whole grains and their brans—including whole wheat, rye, and lesser-known grains such as millet and soy—comprise our best source of dietary fiber, raw fruits and vegetables also supply some. And aside from their fiber content, raw foods also seem helpful in preventing diabetes. Two California physicians, John M. Douglass and Irving Rasgon, have published several reports in medical journals of their successes in controlling diabetes with raw-food therapy. Raw foods, like fibrous foods, move through the system rapidly, and they believe this makes them more advantageous in diabetes control.

Most of us should be concerned about diabetes as we grow older, and we would do well not to consume too much fruit, since fruits contain sugar. Though this sugar is in a form that is easier for the body to handle, it can still create complications if consumed in excess. Drs. Douglass and Rasgon report placing a diabetic on an 80 percent raw-food diet without obtaining any beneficial results. When they looked a little further into the case, they found out that the dieter was eating eighteen bananas a day. Potassium-rich bananas are a healthy food, but eighteen of them was simply shooting too much sugar, albeit fruit sugar, into the patient's system. Almost any health practice can be overdone as was the case here.

IV

You may have heard of chromium, a metal used for many industrial purposes including the manufacture of automobile bumpers. Chromium helps give these bumpers their shiny luster. You may not have heard that chromium is a vital nutrient for human health. This same mineral supplies sheen to auto bumpers and, in a slightly different form, supplies spark to the human body.

The Trace Mineral Laboratory of the Dartmouth Medical School first called attention to the necessity of chromium as a nutrient for proper physiological functioning. The laboratory's founding director, Dr. Henry Schroeder, became intrigued when he found minute amounts of this metal in the bodies of test animals he studied. He began wondering what, if anything, this chromium was doing there. He soon found out that it was doing a lot.

His first experiments consisted of feeding laboratory rats diets deprived of all chromium. The animals, so he and his coworkers observed, soon developed signs of arteriosclerosis, also known as hardening of the arteries. The animals also developed the symptoms of diabetes. When minute amounts of chromium were added to their drinking water, the diabetic symptoms disappeared.

Next came some experiments with humans. A small group of mild diabetics were given chromium supplements, and most, though not all, showed signs of significant improvement. In a test with older diabetics, the response rate was lower. Out of the ten elderly people who were victims of this ailment, six exhibited no benefit from such supplementation.

However, the other four registered a dramatically favorable reaction, for their blood sugar tests became normal.

Other research conducted at Dartmouth and elsewhere began to pour in. One physician examined the hair of a group of diabetic children and found that it contained, on the average, only about two-thirds as much chromium as the hair of nondiabetic youngsters.[2] Others tested undernourished children in Africa and the Near East and found them to have many blood sugar problems. Giving them chromium brought about spectacular improvement, sometimes in as little as eighteen hours. Dr. Schroeder and his Dartmouth colleagues seem to have discovered a valuable dietary element for the prevention and alleviation of diabetes.

Neither Dr. Schroeder nor anyone else could tell at first just how chromium worked its apparent wonders. Further studies led to the theory that this trace mineral activates and potentiates the body's own insulin supply, binding it to those sites in the body where it can do the most good. However, it does not do this directly. Rather it helps create a complex compound that performs this function. Dr. Schroeder christened this compound with the name Glucose Tolerance Factor, a descriptive label that spells out just what it does. The Glucose Tolerance Factor, or GTF, does not consist solely of chromium. It also includes niacin (a form of vitamin B$_3$) and three amino acids. But without chromium no GTF can be formed, and its formation is vital to the task of blood sugar regulation.

How does one obtain chromium? It is not something one can normally purchase in pill form at a drug store or even health-food store, for it is difficult to package the mineral into a tablet that can be easily metabolized by the human body. Usually it has to be obtained by eating foods that contain it.

---

[2]The hair is usually the most convenient site for determining the presence or absence of trace minerals.

The food which furnishes the best source of dietary chromium is probably brewer's yeast, and brewer's yeast in both powdered or tablet forms can be found in nearly all health-food stores. Other dietary sources are liver, black pepper, certain grains, and certain natural sweeteners.

Chromium is found much more abundantly in whole grains than in refined flours. It takes fifteen slices of white bread to provide the amount of chromium found in two slices of whole-wheat bread. The same holds even more true for sweeteners. Blackstrap molasses has more than ten times as much chromium as white sugar, while honey has nearly fifteen times as much.

The result is that white flour and white sugar actually do not add any chromium to the body at all. Instead, they slowly but steadily use up the small amounts we already have. Dr. Schroeder found that refined flours and white sugars helped to deplete the body of chromium over the years, while whole-grain flours, honey, and molasses acted to increase the body's chromium content. Even brown sugar, which is merely white sugar with molasses added, increased body chromium when the sugar was so brown—that is, so saturated with molasses—that it stuck together.

Chromium should not be thought of as a magic elixir that will banish diabetes once and for all. According to Dr. Mark Altshule, it is most effective in adult-onset diabetes, the most common but also the least serious form of the disease. Even here it does not help all cases and works very slowly in those cases it does help. And it does not control diabetes completely.

However, it does offer assistance in alleviating many cases of diabetes and, more importantly, possibly in preventing many more from developing. When we recall that most people, especially most black people, experience difficulties in regulating their blood sugar as they grow older, we can state that every prudent person should make sure that chromium figures in their food supply.

V

Numerous other weapons exist to help us ward off the arrival or curb the effects of diabetes. Some of these are nutritional but some are not.

As regards nutrition, we once again encounter our folklore friend, garlic. You may at first feel that enough magic powers have been ascribed to this plant and that adding an ability to counteract diabetes to its already demonstrated ability to fight high blood pressure and cancer is simply making too much of a good thing. But, as it so happens, garlic has demonstrated a capacity to alleviate diabetic symptoms in test animals under controlled, clinical conditions.

This first came to light in 1973 when three physicians described in *Lancet* a simple but highly significant experiment they had conducted. They had engendered diabetes in rabbits and then brought their blood sugar levels down by feeding them garlic. They had also achieved the same results with onions, which are related to garlic, but it took very substantial quantities of onions to do what much smaller amounts of garlic could accomplish.[3]

Although to my knowledge there have been no clinically controlled tests on the effect of garlic on blood sugar in human beings, the few doctors who have used it in this capacity enthusiastically attest to its effectiveness. Among them is Edgar Lucidi, M.D., a Philadelphia ophthalmologist. (What is an eye specialist, you may be wondering, doing bothering about diabetes? Remember that diabetes is one of the principal causes of blindness as well as other eye problems.)

Dr. Lucidi also has other nutritional recommendations to make, recommendations that lie beyond the pale of everyday medicine as it is currently practiced in the United States.

---

[3] It is also interesting to note that the three physicians had made the rabbits diabetic simply by feeding them sugar. This is another example of how sugar ingestion can by itself create faulty blood sugar functioning.

According to Dr. Lucidi, raw vegetables can dissipate much of the danger which diabetes creates, if not the diabetes itself. He especially recommends string beans and Jerusalem artichokes, both of which, he says, contain "insulin-like factors." He also thinks nonsweet fruits such as grapefruit and lemon are of benefit. And he recommends the consumption of blueberry and juniper-berry teas, both of which are made from the leaves of their respective plants, not from the berries themselves. This last "prescription" for diabetes prevention and/or restriction may sound a bit bizarre, but the leaf of the blueberry plant has long enjoyed a favored place in herbal medicine as a corrective for diabetes.

What about vitamins? Dr. Lucidi recommends a B-complex supplement daily for all diabetics and for those who believe themselves vulnerable to the disease. Here, too, he seems to be standing on safe ground. As another physician, Dr. Mark Altshule of both the Harvard and Yale Medical Schools, has put it, "Some diabetics seem to utilize the B vitamins poorly and do well when receiving an oral B-complex preparation."

The B vitamin that seems most strongly involved with diabetic problems is B_6. Research shows that diabetics have lower amounts of this vitamin in their blood than healthy individuals do, and Dr. Kilmer McCully, another Harvard medical professor, claims that "there is a clear decline of B_6 with age. There is also a dramatic decline of B in diabetics."

There is another aspect of the B_6–diabetic relationship which should interest all health-oriented people, whether or not they consider the illness a personal threat to themselves or those they love. It has been known for some time that pregnancy can trigger diabetes in women who are susceptible to it. Mind you, I said trigger it, not cause it, for if a woman becomes diabetic in pregnancy, she would most probably have developed the disease eventually. It is also known that birth-control pills can have the same effect. The birth-control pill in a sense subjects the woman taking it to what may be called an artificial pregnancy. Both a real pregnancy and the simulated pregnancy provided by the pill can interfere with the body's utilization of Vitamin B_6, and in 1977 research was reported showing that 100 milligrams of B_6, given daily to a group of pregnant women having trouble with blood sugar regulation, improved their condition considerably.

The B vitamins, especially B_6 but the others as well, seem to be the only ones which directly affect diabetic development. However, many of the other vitamins can help modify some of the *consequences* of diabetes. Vitamin E has been known for some time to improve circulation in the extremities, especially the legs. This can be a boon for diabetics who sometimes end up having to have their lower extremities amputated. Vitamin C can also improve circulation, while Vitamin D can help in bone formation. Bone formation normally decreases in diabetics, and animal research opens up the possibility that this decrease can be reduced, possibly even reversed, with adequate amounts of Vitamin D.

What about nonnutritional factors? The evidence indicates that such factors can play a lesser role in preventing and/or alleviating some of the other illnesses which beset black Americans, including diabetes. Tobacco, at least the kind used in most American and European cigarettes, contains a fair amount of sugar, and researchers in Sweden many years ago demonstrated how smoking a cigarette would raise an individual's blood sugar level. Therefore, diabetics or those in danger of developing the disease have an additional reason to refrain from inhaling cigarette smoke.

Stress may also adversely affect diabetes. Some observers say the disease often appears after an incident, an operation, or some other strain to the system. To my knowledge no systematic studies have ever been done to establish this point scientifically, but given the pervasive tendency of stress to create all kinds of medical problems, there is every reason to believe that it can help bring on or aggravate diabetic conditions. And exercise, one of the alleviators of stress, has been found to alleviate diabetes as well, as indicated by some Danish research reported in *The New England Journal of Medicine* in late 1979, which showed that exercise improved the body's utilization of insulin.

As you will perhaps have noticed, most of the measures which scientific study has suggested will help to avert or to alleviate diabetes have also been found helpful in forestalling or easing the effects of other ailments that plague and pester black Americans. Once again we have dramatic demonstration of the fact that the general good health which these measures favor provides the best answer and remains the best antidote for all manner of medical predicaments and problems.

CHAPTER FIVE

Low Blood Sugar

I

You have probably never heard of the Qoola Indians of Bolivia and Peru, but few people have. And before 1973 hardly anyone had. Since that time a small group of scientists, scholars, and interested laypersons have become aware that these simple people can lay claim to a notable but highly dubious distinction: They have the highest homicide rate in the world.

This was first reported by an anthropologist who spent five years living among them. The anthropologist, Dr. Ralph Bolton of Pomona College in Claremont, California, put their homicide rate at 50 per 100,000. To put this in perspective, he added another fact which he had found: 50 percent of the heads of households among this two-million-member group of rural Indians had been directly or indirectly involved in at least one homicide case.

The question that needed answering was why. Why should a population of simple mountain people whose tribal culture and society did not appear to be threatened by any hostile forces from without or within, who seemed, in short, to be living a stable and secure existence, why should such people have become so predisposed to killing one another? Dr. Bolton, who had discovered their penchant for manslaughter and murder, felt once his research was concluded that he had also discovered the answer. He reported that 55 percent of all adult Qoola males suffer either to a high or low degree from hypoglycemia.

Hypoglycemia, whose less scientific name is low blood sugar, earned its status as a bona fide medical malady in the late 1940s. This does not mean that it did not exist before that time, merely that it had not been identified. And it means just what its less scientific title says—that those it afflicts tend to have low levels of glucose, the most basic of all sugars, in their blood.

Why should low blood sugar be such a problem? The reason is that our bodies, generally speaking, and our brains in particular, run on oxygen and sugar. If you shut off the brain's supply of these two commodities, you will render a person unconscious in just ten seconds. Shut off its supply for fifteen or twenty minutes and you will cause irreversible brain damage. A steady stream of oxygen and sugar are essential to maintain the processes of life.

Up to now, I have been treating sugar as if it were nearly poison. Now I am saying that it is the most important substance the body and the brain require. Can this apparent contradiction be explained?

Admittedly, low blood sugar is a puzzling phenomenon at first. Allow me to start my explanation with still another seemingly contradictory statement. *Eating sugar is the worst thing one can do for low blood sugar.* It provides temporary relief only at the price of more severe and longer-lasting problems.

To begin with, let us take note that nearly everything we eat eventually becomes sugar. Food is turned into glucose, a form of sugar, and is carried through our bloodstream to our brains and throughout the rest of our bodies. Solid foods, especially high-protein foods, are converted to glucose at a slow and steady pace. Thus a fairly stable level of glucose is maintained in the blood for fairly long periods of time. But simple carbohydrates, especially refined sugar, are converted rapidly. As a result comparatively large quantities of glucose are injected into the bloodstream rapidly, but once this has been done, the blood sugar level will fall again.

A helpful way to grasp this problem is to remember what happens when you roll up a piece of newspaper and put it on a fire. Suddenly you get a burst of flame and heat, but in a few seconds it will all be over and the fire will be back to where it was before. To obtain a steady supply of light and heat you have to use a log that will burn slowly and less spectacularly.

This is very close to what happens when we consume too many simple starches and sugars and too little protein and complex carbohydrates. Another element enters the picture here. As we saw in the chapter on diabetes, refined sugar and, to a lesser extent, simple starch need insulin to turn them into the glucose that our bodies need. Both, but refined sugar especially, tend to trigger an overproduction of insulin by our hard-working pancreas. The result of so much insulin is a speeding up and intensification of the conversion process, and this soon leaves us with a low level of glucose in the blood.

Looking at its technical name for a moment, hypoglycemia seems to be the exact opposite of diabetes. The latter ailment stems from an inadequate supply of insulin to convert dietary sugar into glucose. Low blood sugar comes from an oversupply of insulin that does its job too well, thereby leaving us with blood sugar levels that are too low rather than too high. Actually, the two illnesses are related: The overstimulation of the insulin-making machinery in the pancreas may eventually cause diabetes. A more immediate effect may be low blood sugar. Viewed from this perspective, low blood

Causes for Controversy

Many differences in opinion among doctors over the incidence of hypoglycemia stem from their different ways of conducting the tests for the illness and of analyzing the results. The standard test for the complaint is administration to the patient of a glucose solution and the drawing of samples of blood. It is recommended that this be done for a full six-hour period, and some claim that the reason why so many doctors have difficulty discovering hypoglycemia is that they don't carry out the testing for the full six-hour period. On the other hand, some doctors insist that the tests prove nothing, since in their view low blood sugar is a perfectly normal response to a quick overload of glucose.

In any case, it is quite easy for you to determine on your own if you may have a predisposition to hypoglycemia. Simply follow the recommended dietary regimen for hypoglycemics for a week or so, as set down in the second section of this chapter. If you feel better as a result, you may well have at least a touch of this malady and therefore may find it wise to continue with the antihypoglycemic diet. The diet, as you will see, can scarcely do you harm, even if you don't have hypoglycemia.

sugar can be regarded as a potential precursor of diabetes. As one health journal puts it, "Low blood sugar and diabetes are two aspects of the same disease. Low blood sugar (hypoglycemia) very often precedes the appearance of diabetes. Once the blood sugar level begins to teeter drastically and change rapidly from high to low, and back to high again, you have a condition that is totally disruptive to everything in your body."

The next question is what has all this to do with the increased propensity to kill people, as witness the seemingly bloodthirsty Qoolas? To quote from the article just mentioned, "Too little sugar [i.e., glucose] in the blood causes the autonomic nervous system to become unbalanced. Blood pressure changes: rapid pulse rate, rapid breathing and sweating are some symptoms of this." There are also many purely emotional effects including "irritability, anxiety, fatigue, temper outbursts and many other symptoms which victims of this disorder know so well."

The question to be asked and, if possible, answered is just how prevalent is this illness in contemporary America? The truth of the matter is that no one can even give a rough estimate with any degree of certainty. Most, though fortunately not all, physicians tend to minimize its incidence. To some degree they are reacting to what they feel are the exaggerations that have been made by "health nuts" and others regarding the evil effects of eating sugar. They also note, with good cause, that the symptoms of hypoglycemia are similar if not actually identical with those of other ailments, including problems that may be strictly emotional in origin and effect. In one study by the highly regarded Mayo Clinic, it was found that of 129 hypoglycemic patients, the majority of them also showed emotional disturbances when given a personality test. In other words, at least part of their problem was mental, not physical.

Physicians who express skepticism as to the pervasiveness of hypoglycemia or low blood sugar claim that many people actually want to be diagnosed as having the ailment. In this way such people can avoid having to face the fact that the problems that beset them are really in their minds and not in their bodies. As one such physician put it, "It is a lot easier to say that you have hypoglycemia than to admit you have an emotional disorder."

There is no question that these physicians have a point. Many nutritionally oriented people have perhaps been too eager to ascribe mental and emotional problems strictly to a disordered diet and to overlook the psychological factors that may be and usually are involved. The tendency is reinforced by the fact that the symptoms of hypoglycemia and many forms of neurosis are similar if not actually the same. It therefore becomes easy to confuse them.

Though the psychological factors and forces which guide and govern behavior must not be neglected, it is nevertheless becoming apparent that nutrition figures into behavior in a much bigger way than most people, including most doctors and mental-health workers, have hitherto suspected. And one of the biggest ways in which dietary intake influences the way we feel and act is through its impact on our blood sugar level.

Those physicians who have taken the illness seriously report finding it to be widespread. A Hollywood, California, psychiatrist, Dr. Harvey Ross, says that his experience convinced him that a full 10 percent of the American population is hypoglycemic. A study in 1974 of approximately 5,000 army inductees found that nearly one-quarter of them (24.4 percent) had hypoglycemia. And Dr. David Hawkins, who heads a publicly funded mental-health center on Long Island, claims his files are bulging with case histories of victims of the illness. They include the cases of a man who lost job after job for fourteen years because of his uncontrollable outbursts and of a woman who spent days staring at a wall and crying.

When investigators test people with pronounced behavioral problems, they often find hypoglycemia to be present. Dr. E. M. Abrahamson, a nutritionally oriented psychiatrist, tested 700 people who were described as "mildly neurotic." The result? Nearly 600 of them had low blood sugar. Dr. Paul J. Dunn, an Oak Park, Illinois, pediatrician tested 144 children who had been diagnosed as "learning disabled." The result? Some 78 percent had low blood sugar. And a group of alcoholics were also given tests for hypoglycemia. The result? Only 3 percent had "normal" levels of blood sugar. One very important thing to bear in mind about low blood sugar is that while it is a chronic ailment for some, it can be an occasional ailment for nearly everyone. All of us can experience temporarily some of its effects if we do not watch what we eat. We may not suffer the deep depressions or bursts of rage of the true hypoglycemic, but we can become moody and/or irritable when our blood sugar levels sink too low. And, don't forget, this is most likely to occur a short time after we have consumed a high-sugar snack unaccompanied by anything else of a more substantial nature.

Now comes the key question, as far as we are concerned, regarding hypoglycemia. How severely does it affect blacks?

There is no definitive answer to this question, for to my knowledge no definitive studies have been done to determine its incidence on a racial basis. However, there are indications that substantially more blacks than whites suffer from hypoglycemia.

The first indicator is the diabetes rate. We have already seen that the incidence of this related illness is appreciably greater among blacks than whites.

A second reason is that blacks, proportionately, are poor, and poor people these days are eating more and more sugary foods, a trend that has been greatly aided and abetted by the federal government's food-stamp program.

The third basis for believing that hypoglycemia is striking blacks more frequently and more severely than whites is that blacks show more signs of the behavioral problems which the illness produces. Violent crime is more common among blacks. So are learning problems, alcoholism, and family breakups. This is not to say that low blood sugar alone is solely or even primarily responsible for the high rate of these emotional problems among blacks. Being black in a nonblack society bestows a burden which, all by itself, can easily cause all kinds of emotional distress. But since low blood sugar so often seems to play a part in such matters, it may well be doing so here.

Hypoglycemia, in short, is no stranger to Black America. It affects blacks as much as and probably more than whites. Reducing its incidence and impact may do much to alleviate and allay a plethora of physical and emotional difficulties that today beleaguer the black community.

Hypoglycemia, despite its far-ranging effects and ominous-sounding name, is fortunately quite easy in most instances to correct. Since its cause is almost always improper diet, its cure or control can usually be effected through diet alone.

The first change the victim must make is replacement of all or nearly all the refined sugar and most of the simple starches in his or her diet with foods high in protein, such as dairy products, nuts, certain legumes (for example, kidney beans and soybeans), and meat and fish. Moderate amounts of fats and complex carbohydrates such as whole grains can also be consumed in most cases, at least eventually if not right away.

It is especially important to eat a high-protein breakfast. The food we start the day with occupies a special place on the agenda of every health-conscious person, but it assumes particular priority for everyone concerned about their blood sugar levels. Back in the early 1960s, researchers at the University of Iowa found that volunteers who ate a high-protein breakfast enjoyed blood sugar levels significantly higher than those whose protein consumption at breakfast was lower. Furthermore, these higher levels were maintained for several hours.

However, other meals are also important, and here the treatment recommended by nearly all doctors is for the patient to break up his or her high-protein diet into five or six small meals each day, rather than two or three big ones. Scattering food intake throughout the day in this fashion provides for a more even flow of glucose into the blood and therefore gives additional insurance against a precipitous drop in blood sugar level. Alcohol, which as we saw earlier is essentially a different and more toxic form of sugar, is usually taboo. Coffee is also frequently banned, and cigarettes may be forbidden as well.

Dr. Robert F. Rogers, a Florida physician who has made a specialty of treating hypoglycemia, contends that "caffeine, nicotine and alcohol stimulate the adrenal glands which push blood sugar out of the liver and into the blood stream." Adds Dr. Rogers, "The quick rise in blood sugar is where the kick of coffee and cigarettes and the euphoria of liquor comes from. But the lift is temporary. When blood sugar plummets, the only way most people can get on top of things is to smoke another cigarette, have another cup of coffee or swig another drink."

Vitamins and minerals do not play any major role, at least directly, in controlling blood sugar, but some of them may be helpful in an ancillary capacity. Dr. Rogers gives his patients supplements of zinc, chromium, and manganese, for he says insulin requires these trace minerals to function properly. He also gives them brewer's yeast. Another physician, W. R. Currier, believes Vitamin C to be useful. Says Dr. Currier, who writes a medical column for a health magazine, "People with low blood sugar almost always have weak adrenal glands and Vitamin C helps compensate for this problem."

III

Some of the great success stories in treating hypoglycemia come from prisons and other incarceration facilities. As noted above, low blood sugar often leads to or adds to antisocial behavior, and many of those convicted of violent crimes have been found to be fully or marginally hypoglycemic. The Institute for Biosocial Research has discovered juvenile offenders who eat as much as 274 pounds of sugar a year, and one or two who consumed 465 pounds a year, well over a pound a day.

Diet and Divorce

Can eating too much sugar lead to divorce? According to some physicians and family therapists, it definitely can.

Dr. Robert L. Rogers of Melbourne, Florida, blames the country's high divorce rate partly on hypoglycemia. Says he, "A husband and wife, both with low blood sugar, who are irritable, moody, anxious and depressed, can't expect to have a happy marriage."

Dr. Mary Lane Hungerford, who directs the Santa Barbara, California, branch of the American Institute of Family Relations, apparently agrees. She says that a full 80 percent of all the troubled spouses who come to her clinic are found to have hypoglycemia and correcting their diet often corrects their marital problems as well.

One person who has put this information to good use is Barbara Reed, chief probation officer for the Municipal Court of Cuyahoga Falls, Ohio. She has found that changing the diet of an offender often does more than any other single step in helping the offender go straight. She almost routinely sends probationers for a glucose-tolerance test, and if it indicates hypoglycemia, she then makes food an integral part of the probationer's rehabilitation program.

Not all the criminals found to have low blood sugar have committed crimes of violence. One woman sent to Ms. Reed was a compulsive shoplifter. She revealed that she frequently ate as much as a pound of candy in one sitting. She also drank coffee compulsively. Nutritional testing revealed not only low blood sugar but mineral imbalances as well. A change in diet produced a speedy and complete change in behavior.

Some, although unfortunately not many, prison psychiatrists have experimented with the use of dietary measures to produce desirable behavioral change. One of them was interviewed by the editor of a newsletter put out by the International Academy of Preventive Medicine. He reported finding that many inmates show signs of hypoglycemia and tend to be impulsive and irritable in their behavior. It is not easy, however, to change their eating habits. "They continue to seek out refined carbohydrates even though they always react to them by becoming upset . . . It has taken us as long as half a year with some persons living under supervision to convince them of their sensitivity to sugar; now they are doing well."

No one but a fanatic, and a rather foolish one at that, would claim that dietary change will give us *the* solution to the problem of crime. But it can contribute, and in many instances contribute mightily, to its reduction. The ancients believed that the body and the mind were linked together in much more than just a physical sense. Modern science is increasingly proving them to have been correct.

IV

In delving into and discussing the various ailments that afflict black Americans with particular severity, we have almost invariably ended up fingering sugar as a major culprit. You may be wondering if sugar is really all that bad. The answer appears to be yes. Not just health faddists but several distinguished doctors, some of them holding teaching posts in well-regarded medical schools, have come to the same conclusion. Simple, refined sugar may well be the most lethal substance on the American dinner table.

At this point it might be useful to review the numerous and nefarious ways in which sugar causes or contributes to poor health. Some of them we have already seen, but others have not yet made an appearance in these pages. Together, they add up to a formidable and fearful indictment.

As we have noted, sugar can be a prime factor in causing diabetes, and it is inevitably the prime factor in causing hypoglycemia. Its ability to rot the teeth is universally accepted. So is its ability to create obesity. It should be noted that sugar tends to do this without regard to mere caloric content alone. Experiments and studies have demonstrated that 100 calories of sugar will add more weight than the same 100 calories consumed in any other food. Calorie for calorie, sugar has shown itself to be far and away the most fattening of foods.

Sugar's peculiar penchant for helping us put on excessive weight probably comes from the fact that it enters the bloodstream so quickly and directly. The body does not burn up any appreciable number of calories in processing sugar. Its pure caloric nature also makes sugar the least fibrous of foods. Indeed, there is virtually no bulk or roughage to refined sugar at all.

Sugar has also been definitely shown to impair the body's immune system. This has been noted earlier in this book and deserves to be continually emphasized since, regrettably, this fact seems to be little known or little appreciated by most doctors or other health practitioners. There is no controversy surrounding the research which shows sugar to have this effect. Tests have repeatedly confirmed it. Rather, this important information has simply been ignored. And since we rely on our immune systems to help us ward off a variety of ills ranging from colds to cancer, we can ignore sugar's debilitating effect on it only at our peril.

Even less well known is sugar's effect on the vitamins and minerals we consume. Sugar tends to destroy the B vitamins and to flush such valuable minerals as magnesium and zinc out of our systems. Chromium, too, as Dr. Schroeder found out, is gradually stripped from our bodies through ingestion of refined sugar.

Sugar has also been found to enhance the effect of salt in boosting blood pressure. A research physician at the Louisiana State University Medical School discovered this some years ago. He found that simultaneously feeding monkeys sugar and salt elevated their blood pressure much higher than feeding them salt alone, and the additional rise was not connected with any additional gain in weight.

Finally, even those of us who would not be diagnosed as having hypoglycemia can suffer from the "hyped-up highs," followed by the sudden and sharp lows which sugar eating can create. As a writer in *Essence* put it, "That rush of energy you get as you ingest refined sugar is a false high. The rapid increase of glucose into your bloodstream will make you feel energized, true, but it really is overtaxing your system, forcing your body to compensate, leaving you tired later on. It's then that your body crashes. What is distressing is the cycle it sends us on. After the crash, we reach for another soft drink, another cookie to pick us up . . ."

Yes, sugar is a "no-no," perhaps the ultimate dietary "no-no" for those who wish to live long and vigorous lives. Brown sugar is a bit better than white sugar, but the difference is not significant because brown sugar is merely white sugar coated with molasses. This does add slight quantities of other nutrients—it will be recalled that very brown sugar, that is,

TABLE 4
How Sweet It Is

Food Item	Portion Size	Teaspoons of Sugar (approx.)
Soda	8 oz.	5
Angel cake	4 oz.	7
Chocolate cake (iced)	4 oz.	10
Sponge cake	4 oz.	8
Coffee cake	4 oz.	4½
Cupcake (iced)	1	6

sugar that has been deeply coated with molasses, will not deprive the body of chromium—but what it adds is rarely very substantial. Honey, molasses, and maple syrup are certainly less harmful, and the first two, in limited quantities, may well be health enhancing.[1]

Honey, molasses, and maple syrup all represent sugar as it is found in nature itself. It is not without interest, and possibly not without importance, that even the cane sugar which we more commonly consume does not seem to have many harmful effects *in its natural state.* Sugar-cane cutters munch freely and often continually on sugar canes, yet they usually possess cavity-free teeth and diabetes-free bodies. But the sugar they are ingesting comes mixed in with other food substances, as it comes in honey, molasses, and maple syrup. Nothing in nature comes in a pure state, and pure sugar may, in its way, be one of the world's greatest dietary impurities.

---

[1]Maple syrup is sugar in the same basic form (sucrose) as table sugar, but it does contain some other factors, including potassium. Make sure when you are buying it that it is real maple syrup and not one of the numerous and almost totally artificial substitutes which currently glut the market.

CHAPTER SIX

Sickle-Cell Anemia, Iron-Deficiency Anemia, and Systemic Lupus Erythematosus

I

Sickle-cell anemia is the ailment most closely and most exclusively associated with black America. Approximately one out of twelve American blacks carries the sickle-cell trait, while one in every six hundred suffers from sickle-cell anemia itself. A few whites, virtually all of them of Mediterranean ancestry, suffer from the disease, but over 95 percent of all sickle-cell victims are black.

The malady gets its name from the form which the red blood cells assume in those it strikes. These cells, whenever they become short of oxygen, tend to change shape. Normally such cells resemble a wheel, but a sickle cell, when the conditions are right, takes on the shape of a bizarre, elongated crescent. It is as though the cell had been pried open. This new crescent-like configuration reminded the researchers who first discovered it of a farmer's sickle. Hence the name sickle-cell anemia. The problems these deformed cells produce derive from the fact that they tend to stick together, thereby clogging the blood vessels and interrupting the flow of oxygen to the blood. When it recognizes these cells, the spleen will seek to stamp them out, but this seemingly beneficial action may only deprive the victim of his or her full quota of red blood cells.

Although the sickle cell in present day America causes death to some and discomfort to many others, it originally provided protection. While the process is as yet far from fully understood, it appears that the factors which foster it also tend to foster resistance to malaria. Thus, for a person living in central Africa, having sickle cells was a great advantage. But, you may now be asking, if sickle cells did confer some immunity to malaria, why did they also cause anemia? We will examine an intriguing aspect of that question shortly.

Those with 30 percent sickle cells are considered to have the trait while those with 80 percent sickle cells are judged as suffering from the anemia. In between there are some borderline cases consisting of people half of whose cells are susceptible. For those who have the trait, the consequences are customarily not too critical. To be sure, they must take precautions to avoid situations where oxygen may be in short supply. This would normally include pilot training, and the United States Air Force Academy screens out all recruits with the sickle-cell trait. But travel in regular passenger planes is okay since a steady oxygen supply in such airliners is maintained. Deep-sea diving may also prove troublesome to those carrying the sickle-cell trait, and some may occasionally experience problems when engaged in any highly strenuous activity that greatly increases the body's need for oxygen. But most trait carriers can expect to enjoy reasonably long and nearly normal lives if they take reasonable precautions.

For those whose red blood cells are more than 50 percent sickle cells, the effects are usually far more serious.

The first symptoms of sickle-cell anemia may be noticed a few months after birth. Babies suffering from this form of anemia tend to be irritable and colicky and to cry easily. Swelling of the hands and feet is also common. As they get older, such children will frequently experience severe pain in their arms and legs, usually accompanied by fever. A yellow color about the eyes and a protruding pot belly are common. The child will seem lethargic and complain of not having any energy.

As adults, sickle-cell-anemia sufferers may experience a gamut of ills including leg ulcers, blood in the urine, low resistance to fevers, and general weakness. However, these complaints are not constant. The patient will almost always experience periods, and often long periods, of nearly normal living. But periodically there will be "crises" which can cause a great deal of suffering and even death. Pregnancy and surgery are especially hazardous.

One occasional symptom of this ailment in males is what is called priapism, a condition characterized by an erection which will not go down. This condition, which is caused by a blockage of the blood to the penis, can occur in children as young as five years old as well as in adults. There have been cases where such erections lasted twenty to thirty days. Fortunately, such priapism is not a common occurrence.

Developed in response to and in resistance to malaria, the sickle cell has become a mutation that is passed genetically from one generation to another. If both parents have the trait, then for each child the chances are one in four of having sickle-cell anemia, one in two of simply having the trait, and one in four of having completely normal red blood cells. If only one parent has the trait, then there is a 50–50 chance for each child to have the trait but no chance for any child to develop the anemia. Such are the iron laws of inheritance when it comes to the once protective and now pernicious sickle cell.

II

Although the sickle cell and the anemia it can cause were identified in 1910, the search for a solution lagged until 1972. It was in that year that Congress passed and President Nixon signed into law a bill creating the Sickle-Cell Disease Branch of the National Institutes of Health. Since that time research into the disease has proceeded apace. As of this writing no particular drug has been developed to deal with the disease in any decisive way. However, some research being carried on at the Massachusetts Institute of Technology and at the Weizmann Institute of Science in Israel has yielded some promising signs. This research has centered on a class of compounds, called amino-acid benzyl esters, which demonstrates some ability to penetrate red cells and prevent the structural distortions which characterize the sickle cell.

In the meantime, much progress has been made in testing for the sickle cell, to the point where doctors can determine whether an unborn fetus will have sickle-cell anemia, or the trait, or normal red blood cells. Furthermore, some nutrients have been found to be potentially helpful in mitigating the effects of the sickle cell. These involve principally one trace mineral and two vitamins.

Since the early 1950s, researchers have known that those who have sickle cells also show signs of needing increased amounts of folic acid. Folic acid, or folacin as it is sometimes called, is a B vitamin which has been the subject of a good deal of scientific scrutiny in recent years. It is known that it plays a critical role in the functioning of the immune system and so could assist quite possibly those whose immune systems have been weakened by sickle-cell anemia or by the sickle-cell trait.

A still more promising vitamin and one about which more actual research has been done in this connection is

Sickle-Cell Treatment Centers

Northeast

Boston City Hospital
818 Harrison Ave.
Boston, MA 02118
(617) 424-5727

St. Luke's Hospital Center
419 W. 114th Street, Room 403
New York, NY 10025
(212) 870-1756

South

Howard University
2121 Georgia Ave., NW
Washington, DC 20059
(202) 636-7930

Medical College of Georgia
1435 Lancy Walker Blvd.
Augusta, GA 30912
(404) 828-3091

Midwest

University of Illinois
1959 West Taylor Stree
Chicago, IL 60612
(312) 996-7013

University of Chicago
950 East 59th St.
Chicago, IL 60637
(312) 947-5501

Children's Hospital of Michigan
3901 Beaubien Blvd.
Detroit, MI 48201
(313) 494-5611

Children's Hospital Medical Center
Elland and Bethesda Ave.
Cincinnati, OH 45229
(513) 559-4534

West

San Francisco General Hospital
1001 Potrero Ave.
San Francisco, CA 94110
(415) 821-5169

University of Southern California
1129 N. State St., Trailer 12
Los Angeles, CA 90033
(213) 226-3653

If there is no treatment center near you
or if you wish other information, write:

Sickle Cell Disease Branch
National Heart, Lung and Blood Institute
Federal Building
7550 Wisconsin Ave.
Bethesda, MD 20205

Vitamin E. Some investigators have long believed this vitamin to be helpful in assisting the body in utilizing oxygen, and, as we saw earlier, sickle cells interfere with the oxygenation process, thereby increasing the body's oxygen re-

> ## Sickle-Cell Anemia:
> ## One Woman's Story
>
> Jacklyn McDonald was nine months old when doctors discovered that she had sickle-cell anemia. They predicted that she would die before her sixth birthday. They had also made the same prediction for her similarly afflicted sister who was then five years old.
>
> Today, Jacklyn is 27 and her sister is 32, but it hasn't been easy. Jacklyn has periodically suffered through crises which forced her to forfeit her profession as a teacher and even wreaked havoc with her efforts to support herself as a secretary. Nevertheless she has survived and is now a freelance writer living in Brooklyn. She realizes that she is not physically strong enough to bear children, but hopes to get married, as her sister has done, and adopt some.
>
> Jacklyn McDonald is no quitter. She knows that research is steadily going on to discover new and better ways of treating her illness. In the meantime, as she puts it in the conclusion of an article she wrote for *Essence* magazine, "I can't give up. I have things to do, places to go. I plan to live a long, full life."

quirements. Thus, anything that could enable the system to process oxygen more efficiently could help alleviate some of the effects of the sickle cell.

In 1965 two medical researchers at Columbia University reported finding widespread Vitamin-E deficiencies among a group of sickle-cell-anemia patients when compared with a control group that did not have this illness. This alone suggests that the system could be using, and thereby using up, the vitamin in trying to combat the disease. In 1979 a research team from the Children's Hospital Medical Center in Oakland, California, also reported finding low Vitamin-E levels in the blood of sickle-cell patients. Based on this discovery, they theorized that taking supplements of this vitamin might help stabilize the red blood cells of such patients and make those cells more resistant to sickling. As one member of the medical team pointed out, although as many as 80 percent of the cells of a sickle-cell-anemia sufferer may sickle, most of them will do so only under certain circumstances. Supplying Vitamin E might improve the cells' ability to withstand those conditions which tend to produce the sickling.

Zinc is the mineral which at this writing appears to hold some hope for those afflicted with this ailment. Here again the starting point was the discovery of an unusual deficiency, for while most Americans tend to be deficient in zinc these days, those with the sickle-cell syndrome seem significantly more deficient in this vital trace mineral than are others. Based on this finding, Dr. George F. Brewer, a physician on the faculty of the University of Michigan, has begun using zinc therapy with some initially encouraging results. Taking one young man whose life seemed in jeopardy, Dr. Brewer had him take a zinc supplement six times a day. He was to take the zinc between meals to aid its absorption, for unlike vitamins which need food to be present in the stomach in order to be fully absorbed, minerals, or at least this mineral, are better utilized when the stomach is empty. The young patient's daily zinc intake under Dr. Brewer's schedule came to 267 milligrams per day, which is a large dose of any trace mineral. It seemed to be effective, for the youth whose life was in danger managed to get through the following three months without a crisis. However, while most black Americans—or, for that matter, most all Americans—could add zinc to their diet with only beneficial results, no one should take as much as Dr. Brewer's patient without a doctor's supervision.

Cyanate is another dietary ingredient to be considered when it comes to combating sickle-cell anemia, and this may be the most decisive one of all, as we shall see.

The sickle-cell phenomenon developed as a way of resisting malaria. But if it did prove useful in this regard, what about its less attractive aspects? If it prevented malaria, wasn't this achieved only at the cost of causing anemia?

Here we come to an intriguing element in the sickle-cell story. In Africa, it is estimated that 25 percent of a population of three-hundred million carry the sickle-cell trait.

Given the statistics noted earlier on the likelihood of the disease developing when two people with the trait marry and have children, one would expect to find millions of cases of sickle-cell anemia. Yet it happens that the disease in Africa is quite rare. From 1925 to 1950, for example, less than one-hundred cases of the anemia were reported throughout the continent. Furthermore, the seventy-odd millions who carry the trait show, for the most part, no signs of disability even under the most strenuous situations. Why? Writing in the *American Journal of Clinical Nutrition* in 1974, scientist Robert G. Huston came up with a reason. Several of the ordinary foods consumed by Africans contain rich sources of cyanate, and cyanate, he said, seems to have a strong inhibiting effect on cell sickling.

Cyanate is a fairly close relative to a deadly poison called cyanide. But despite its similarity in chemical structure to cyanide, cyanate is normally considered nontoxic. In the early 1970s a research team from Rockefeller University and Cornell University Medical Center did some test-tube studies on the effect of cyanate on the sickling process. They then followed this with a six-month study of cyanate on a group of volunteers. In April 1972 the group's leader and spokesman, Dr. Anthony Cerami, told a scientific conference about finding cyanate to be safe and effective in inhibiting the sickling process, but he emphasized that it would not cure the problem. Those suffering from the disease would have to take cyanate for the rest of their lives.

Interest in cyanate understandably perked up at this disclosure, but by the mid- or late 1970s, it had subsided. The reason is that cyanate is closely related to laetrile, the highly controversial drug. As a matter of fact, laetrile is a form of cyanate. And the medical establishment's desire to discredit laetrile as a cure for cancer cut short efforts to develop the same pharmacological principle as a control for sickle-cell anemia.

Fortunately, cyanate is obtainable from food. The

average African, estimates Huston, obtains 1,000 milligrams of cyanate a day in his diet. The average Afro–American ingests a mere 25 milligrams each day. Where does the native African get his cyanate? Principally from yams and cassava plants, says scientist Huston, although millet and sorghum also help provide this valuable nutrient. Cabbage, kidney beans, lentils, other legumes, and the seeds of many fruits are additional sources of cyanate. Consequently, while it may be difficult if not impossible for the average Afro–American to duplicate the diet of his or her forebears, he or she can, with a little ingenuity, come up with alternate sources of cyanate. Those Afro–Americans who have sickle-cell anemia, as well as those who only carry the trait, should make an effort to include cyanate-yielding foods in their daily diet. Such foods, along with Vitamin-E, zinc, and folic-acid supplementation, may be of great assistance in dealing with the dangerous and often disabling effects of the sickle cell.

III

The term anemia commonly designates virtually any deficiency in the number and/or activity of the red blood cells. As such, it is applied to a large number of ailments, the most common of which is iron-deficiency anemia.

Iron deficiencies in American women and children of all races are far from rare. A 1974 study by the Department of Health, Education and Welfare found that nearly 95 percent of all American women in the 18 to 44 age group were iron deficient. Their daily iron intake averaged only 10½ milligrams versus the recommended intake of 18 milligrams per day. They are thus getting only 58 percent of the iron they should be getting in their diet. And while not every person who lacks iron is anemic, an iron deficiency puts anyone in danger of becoming so. Indeed, any lack of iron will, if carried too far and too long, almost inevitably produce anemia.

The most common symptom of an iron deficiency, and especially of anemia itself, is fatigue. The victim tires easily and quickly. Other symptoms include irritability, headaches, shortness of breath (especially upon exertion), gas, indigestion, and lack of coordination. It should come as no surprise that many of the symptoms of iron-deficiency anemia parallel those of sickle-cell anemia. In both cases, the blood is not getting all the oxygen it needs. In the case of the sickle cell, this is caused principally by the clogging action of the distended cells; in the case of iron deficiency, it is caused by a lack of iron which the blood needs to bind the oxygen to it. In the more severe stages of iron-deficiency anemia, the heart may enlarge as it desperately tries to supply oxygen to the iron-lacking, and therefore oxygen-losing, red blood cells.

Unlike sickle-cell anemia, iron-deficiency anemia is fairly common among whites but twice as common among blacks. In both races it primarily strikes women in their childbearing years who lose substantial amounts of iron during menstruation. However, it can affect children as well. (Incidentally, one common sign of iron deficiency in children is an unusually sharp desire to suck on ice.) In any case, one should keep in mind that a mild iron deficiency, while it should certainly be corrected, is still a far cry from full-fledged anemia.

Why black women should be more iron deficient than white women is not fully known. Of course, the average white female is richer than her black sister and therefore has greater recourse to meats and other good sources of iron. Her greater wealth may also give her access to still other foods whose vitamin content enhances the system's ability to absorb iron. One more explanation is offered by a black physician in Queens, New York. Dr. Gerald Deas, who holds a master's degree in public health in addition to his doctorate in medicine, believes laundry starch may supply part of the answer. He says that so many of his black patients eat laundry starch that he no longer asks them whether they do so but only how much they consume. He estimates that two million American blacks have an insatiable craving for such starch which, because it tends to bind iron and make it unavailable to the body, can cause anemia.

The cause of this craving remains speculative. Dr. Deas believes it comes from its corn-like crunchiness. Nutritionist Carlton Fredericks wonders whether or not it may signify a hidden food allergy. Regardless of the reason, if two million or even one million blacks are consuming substantial quantities of laundry starch, iron-deficiency problems are certain to arise.

When it comes to curing such a deficiency one normally thinks of iron supplements, and most doctors prescribe such supplements routinely for those suffering from too little iron. But the problem is not just ingesting enough iron but in absorbing and assimilating it. Normally we absorb only about 10 percent of the iron we consume. This absorption rate can be greatly boosted, however, with the addition of Vitamin C. Studies at Georgetown University and at a Minneapolis hospital have revealed remarkable success in increasing the iron-absorption rate by adding Vitamin C to the diet. The vitamin does not necessarily need to be taken in tablet form in order for its beneficial effects to be realized. Often just including some foods naturally rich in Vitamin C will substantially step up the system's utilization of the iron supplied by the other foods ingested at the same time. This is one reason why liver is such a good source of iron, for it actually contains Vitamin C as well as iron itself. Liver also contains numerous other vitamins that can, in one way or another, help protect the system from anemia.

One such vitamin is B_{12}, an important aid in generally toning up the body. In Europe, doctors frequently give their run-down patients injections of Vitamin B_{12} to give them more pep. Another B vitamin which is found in liver and which has been found to have some role in preventing anemia is folic acid. Anemic patients often show low levels of this vitamin in their blood. Folic acid was also found to be frequently in short supply in sickle-cell anemia patients. So was Vitamin E. And just as Vitamin E showed signs of being helpful to sickle-cell-anemia patients, so may it also be of use to those suffering from more common forms of anemia. Vitamin E's apparent ability to assist the system in utilizing oxygen could be responsible for its role in alleviating anemia. Although this role remains somewhat disputed, a string of studies going back to the 1950s demonstrates that anemia can be produced in test animals and in young men by making them deficient in Vitamin E. With this in mind, all black Americans, male or female, should make sure to get enough Vitamin E. Certain vegetable oils, especially wheat-germ oil, contain Vitamin E, providing they have not been heated or hydrogenated. Leafy, green vegetables and whole grains also contain this vitamin and, of course, it can be obtained in tablet form.

One final note: Iron in its inorganic form actually tends to destroy Vitamin E in the system, and, unfortunately, most of the iron found in iron supplements is in this form. Thus, if you are taking iron supplements, do not take your Vitamin E at the same time. Put at least six hours between the time you take one and the time you take the other. Otherwise much of the Vitamin E you take will be lost.

IV

Although much less well known than sickle-cell anemia, systemic lupus erythematosus (also known as SLE or lupus) is another illness which seems to have made American blacks its favorite target. And since it tends to strike women almost ten times as often as men, it poses a special danger to black women. One San Francisco study found 1 in every 245 black females suffering from systemic lupus erythematosus. However, as with hypoglycemia and diabetes, many who have this illness do not know they have it.

One reason why SLE often goes so long without being properly diagnosed by either the victim or doctor is that its symptoms tend to duplicate those of other illnesses. These symptoms may include fevers, headaches, infections, hair loss, lesions on the hands, and nodules under the arms. The symptoms are usually intermittent rather than constant, and this may also trick the victim into believing that what was wrong has passed. Sooner or later, though, the same or other symptoms will return.

While lupus has been receiving increasing attention from the research community in recent years, its causes still remain something of a medical mystery. Its basic origin is believed to be genetic, for investigators have found, among other things, that if one twin comes down with the disease, there is a 50 to 60 percent chance that the other twin will follow suit. Ultraviolet rays are believed to have some effect in activating or aggravating it. Infections may also cause it to flare up.

Lupus frequently focuses much of its destructiveness on the kidneys. However, it can also harm the heart and brain and can even cause death. Fortunately, while modern medicine still doesn't know all that much about the illness, it nevertheless has developed some strategies for dealing with it. Twenty-five years ago barely one-half those who came down with it could expect to be alive five years later; today over 90 percent can expect to meet that goal. To a considerable extent, lupus can be controlled, though not cured, by drugs—primarily by a drug known as prednisone. Unfortunately, this drug can cause some unpleasant side effects, including an increased disposition to gain weight.

If the diagnosis can be made early enough, and the SLE victim faithfully follows doctor's orders, then she or he can look forward to a normal or nearly normal life span. In the

What Is the Outlook for SLE?

Although the ultimate cure for SLE must await further knowledge of its basic cause, presently available forms of treatment can effectively hold back, for a significant time, the grave changes that often occur in the disease. In the last few years, good progress has been made toward understanding the way SLE develops, and the outlook is better than previously thought. Currently, great effort is being expended to study in depth in laboratory animals diseases very similar to SLE. Colonies of these animals have been bred to provide all-important experimental models for laboratory investigation.

Genetic studies relating the occurrence of SLE to heredity have begun to yield important information. Also, the study of immunity—the condition of being able to resist disease—is pointing the way to an understanding of the relationship of abnormal antibody production to SLE.

The prevention of disability, the control of fatal complications, and prolonged survival for all those afflicted are the inevitable dividends of the massive research program aimed at systemic lupus erythematosus. Although much remains to be done, much has been accomplished.

Source: From Systemic Lupus Erythematosus, a fact sheet issued by the U.S. Department of Health, Education and Welfare, 1979.

meantime, anyone concerned with avoiding the illness should also avoid excessive exposure to strong sunlight or to strong fluorescent lights such as those found in shopping centers. They should also try to avoid colds and other types of infections.

Are there any dietary devices for sidestepping lupus or for suppressing it if it has already struck? So far no research has arisen directly connecting the ailment to any nutritional cause or indicating any nutritional therapy. However, two vitamins could possibly be of benefit.

One of these is Vitamin C. As noted in Chapter Three, this vitamin has demonstrated some definite ability to enhance the immune system. Since SLE does appear to have some special sensitivity to infectious agents, bolstering this system could be of benefit in warding off or withstanding it.

The second vitamin that might possibly be of use in

dealing with SLE is Vitamin E. As already stated, no scientific study links this or any other nutrient to this illness, but we do have evidence linking Vitamin E to a related disorder known as discord lupus erythematosus (DLE). DLE has more in common with SLE than part of its name. It is also a virus-type illness which attacks the human body. However, while SLE breaks down connective tissue, DLE tends to strike the skin, producing red blotches and plaques.

Samuel Ayres, M.D., and Richard Mihan, M.D., Los Angeles dermatologists associated with the UCLA Medical School, claim to have achieved excellent results using Vitamin E to combat DLE. They stress that the vitamin must be used in very high doses (1,200 to 1,800 units a day) to register results. And sometimes this therapy must be supplemented with selenium, a trace mineral which has a host of beneficial uses, including the activation and potentiation of Vitamin E. But used in this way, the vitamin, so the physicians assert, has proven to be a most productive way of treating DLE. This does not mean that it would work the same wonders for its sister ailment, SLE. The latter is a more destructive disease, and, in any case, Vitamin E has in other studies shown itself to have a special influence on skin. On this account, it might be of more value in controlling DLE than SLE.

On the other hand, Vitamin E is readily available and has a variety of uses. Furthermore, it is known that the average American, black or white, obtains in his or her daily diet only about one-half the 15 units of Vitamin E which the conservative Food and Nutrition Board recommends as a proper dosage. Furthermore, according to Drs. Ayres and Mihan, who have published other research on the vitamin, it is easily destroyed by many staples of modern life. "Unsaturated fats, laxatives and mineral oil, inorganic iron, white bread and cereals 'enriched' with iron, and estrogen exert an antagonistic effect on the utilization of vitamin E," they say.

With these facts in mind, as well as the other research cited previously to point out the vitamin's possible utility in enhancing health, the prudent reader will do well to make it part of his or her anti-SLE regimen, as well as his or her general health-enhancing program.

CHAPTER SEVEN

Toward a Healthier Black America

I

Although the "developed" world likes to think of itself as far ahead of the "underdeveloped" world, this century has seen numerous instances where White Europe and America have looked to Black Africa for instruction and inspiration. As noted earlier, much of modern art, including the famed Cubist movement, came about only when Picasso and other master artists of the West began to study African sculpture. In similar fashion, many, indeed most, of the more exciting developments in Western music owe their origins to the African rhythms and music patterns out of which Afro–Americans created the Negro spiritual and jazz. And much of modern dance, including tap dance, must be credited to Africans and their descendants living in the West.

Now health seems to have joined the fold. Thanks to the discoveries of Dr. Dennis Burkitt and other British physicians, the West is once again looking to the dark continent for enlightenment. More and more Western experts believe they have found one of the keys to health in the basic African diet.

In one sense it is as nonsensical to talk of the "basic African diet" as it is to speak of the basic European diet. The food intake of, say, a Masai tribesman living in East Africa will differ as much, if not more, from that of an urbanized Ibo on the western coast as will the diet of an Italian peasant from that of a Swedish bank clerk. Yet certain common factors do tend to characterize the nutritional patterns of many Africans, and more and more of the wiser health watchers in Europe and America are seeking to adopt them. If duplicating, at least in part, the basic African diet makes sense for a Western white, it certainly makes much more sense for a Western black. Thus, the first and perhaps most significant step which black Americans can take to help their health is, in effect, to come home.

Black America—and White America, too, for that matter—need to come home to a diet centered largely, though not exclusively, on three fundamental food groups: fruits, vegetables, and whole grains. A mounting pile of evidence points to these three basic types of foods as the prime promoters of that maximum state of physical and mental well-being which the World Health Organization defines as good health.

A diet founded on these foods will do more than simply help black Americans avoid or alleviate some of the ills that seem to strike them with somewhat greater frequency or intensity than such ills attack whites. They will also provide protection against an assortment of other ailments. For example, fibrous foods, as we saw in Chapters Two, Three, and Four, can do a great deal to hold down weight, prevent cancer of the digestive tract, and avert, or at least soften the severity of, diabetes. Africans who make such foods the mainstay of their diets rarely suffer from such illnesses. At the same time, they also are rarely afflicted with appendicitis, varicose veins, constipation, hemorrhoids, ulcers, or diaphragmatic hernias, all ailments common to Westerners of all races. Dr. Burkitt and his associates became convinced that high-fiber diets protected their patients against these complaints. Just straining during bowel movements, an all-too-common practice among people who eat too much processed food, can produce such ills, says Dr. Burkitt, while the Africans he studied, who moved their bowels comfortably twice a day, had hardly ever heard of such problems.

But while the basic African eating pattern does provide the basis for a healthy diet for modern-day Afro–Americans, it does require some supplementation and modification to ensure maximum health. For one thing, black Americans could well use a bit more protein than the native African diet customarily provides.

Protein can be obtained from several sources, but for various reasons, some of these sources are far better than others. Among the best sources are organ meats and fish. Organ meats are cuts from various organs of an animal's body, such as the liver, kidney, brain, or heart. All these organs make for healthy eating. This is especially true for liver, which stands out as a veritable treasure trove of valuable nutrients. In addition to many vitamins and minerals, these include the cell-building substance known as ribonucleic acid. As a matter of fact, liver seems to contain some invigorating ingredients that have yet to be fully identified. It deserves a prominent place on any health-conscious person's menu.

Although most people think only of beef liver or calf's liver, other kinds are available. Chopped chicken liver is a delicacy favored among Jewish people, and even many non-Jews find it as tasty as it is nutritious. Pork liver, while less well known than other kinds, also has a lot to offer. It is, for one thing, the richest source of iron of any known food.

The other organ meats, while scarcely staples of the average American diet, are fairly popular foods in many

TABLE 5
The National Academy of Science's Recommended Daily Allowances for Protein

Group	Age	RDA
Children	1–3	23 grams
Children	4–6	30 grams
Children	7–10	36 grams
Males	11–14	44 grams
Males	15–22	54 grams
Males	23 and over	56 grams
Females	11–14	44 grams
Females	19 and over	48 grams
Pregnant women		Add 30 grams
Lactating women		Add 20 grams

European countries. I can personally recall eating kidneys three nights in a row in France and finding them to be differently, and deliciously, prepared on each occasion. And kidneys, while perhaps not quite in liver's class when it comes to nutritional value—almost no food is—can nevertheless be classified as a most nourishing protein source.

Fish is another foodstuff which provides protein accompanied with many additional nutritional assets. Some of the most easily available and commonly consumed kinds of fish are among the most nourishing. Sardines, which contain much nucleic acid, herring, which harbors a lot of zinc, and tuna, which is a good source of the valuable trace mineral selenium, fall into this category. Some kinds of fish contain a lot of salt, so check the table in the Appendix before buying at the fish counter. Also, any canned fish will almost certainly be packed with a great deal of added salt and should be washed thoroughly before being eaten.

Although organ meats and fish are by far the most healthful of the flesh foods, many of the others can be eaten as well. As a general guideline when it comes to meat, chicken is better than lamb, lamb is better than pork, and pork is better than beef. Placing beef last may surprise you, but this popular meat is unquestionably the most harmful. First, it has the highest fat content of all meats. Second, it contains substantial amounts of a powerful cancer-causing substance known to chemists as malonaldrahyde. As a result, beef consumption correlates throughout the world, and correlates strongly, with cancer, especially cancer of the bowel and colon.[1]

One should also not forget nonflesh sources of protein such as eggs, dairy products, and certain plant foods, most notably beans. There is plenty of protein available for everyone, and no one needs to be deprived of this vital, cell-building nutrient. At the same time, one would do well not to go overboard in ingesting protein. Animals fed high-protein diets frequently show increased susceptibility to cancer and almost always die sooner than those fed a more balanced regimen. Large amounts of protein also place extra stress on the kidneys (meat protein in particular). Consequently, while we should make sure to get enough protein, we should also exercise caution about getting too much.

The foods to be minimized or avoided altogether are not many, but they are unfortunately all too deeply imbedded in the nutritional pattern of American life. Two of these, as you already know, are sugar and salt. As documented in earlier chapters, these two "food enhancers" can create a deluge of deleterious effects, especially, so it seems, for those of African ancestry.

Fortunately, more-than-adequate substitutes can be

---

[1]The National Cancer Institute has compiled some truly alarming figures on this, but it has done little to publicize them. Thus the nation's powerful beef industry continues to promote its products with little or no confrontation.

found to replace them. For sugar there are honey, molasses, and maple syrup. While none of them, especially maple syrup, should be eaten in excess, they can all be conservatively consumed by healthy people without any anticipation of adverse effects. On the contrary, the evidence suggests that eaten in moderate amounts, such sweeteners, especially honey and molasses, may be of nutritional benefit.

Artificial sweeteners such as saccharine are another story. They certainly bestow no benefits and, in excessive amounts, could possibly do some harm. Yet the sum and substance of the evidence indicate that moderate ingestion poses no real peril to the average consumer. Since they do not add extra weight, weaken the immune system, force the insulin-pumping pancreas to work overtime, or produce any of the other ill effects associated with refined sugar, they may in moderate amounts be advantageously substituted for sugar.

Substitutes for salt are also readily available. The first of these are the condiments labeled "salt substitute," which are sold in health-food stores and some supermarkets. These usually consist of potassium chloride, and this makes them doubly desirable since they replace sodium in the system with its natural enemy, potassium. The taste of these salt substitutes does take some getting used to, but most people who continue using them ultimately find them quite acceptable.

More satisfactory substitutes for salt may be found on the spice rack. Sage, thyme, paprika, dill, cayenne—these and an abundance of others can be used to make dishes more palatable and pleasing. What's more, many of them, in contrast to salt, can actually improve health rather than impair it. They can be utilized in all kinds of ways. Chili powder and paprika can be sprinkled on eggs instead of salt; basil and thyme can be dashed over tomatoes; and so on. Here is a chance to use your ingenuity to concoct ways to cook with a minimum of salt. And don't be afraid to substitute a small spice rack for the salt shaker on the dinner table.

Another mainstay of the modern Western diet which Afro–Americans should consume in only minimal amounts is white flour. In a sense, this has already been noted, for in underscoring the desirability of whole grains, one at least implicitly condemns processed grains, of which white flour is the most common and most calamitous example. But the case against white flour should be spelled out in some detail so that its full dimensions can be appreciated.

When wheat flour is processed into white flour, over thirty vitamins and minerals are destroyed in whole or in part. A few of the vitamins are then partially put back in synthetic form. This is the basis for the totally absurd claim made by the food companies that their white flour has been "enriched." But the majority of the nutrients are not restored at all. Thus, white flour has less than one-fifth of the magnesium, chromium, zinc, selenium, and other minerals of the whole wheat from which it has been made.

Most of the white flour used in modern cooking has also been bleached. A chlorine compound is usually used to do this, and such a compound is classified by chemists as an oxidant. These oxidants are those compounds whose presence in the atmosphere tends to make iron rust and to make fats rancid. Biochemists working in this field have been accumulating evidence to show that oxidants also tend to make us age more rapidly. Consequently, the chlorine dioxide used to bleach white flour can scarcely be looked upon as a nutritional blessing.

Switching to whole-grain flours may take a bit of doing. But, as anyone who has done it will agree, the results are eventually rewarding to health and to taste. Anyone who has given up white flour for a while will almost always find upon eating it once again that it seems like a doughy, tasteless glue which, as it so happens, is what it is—white flour and water mixed together produce a perfect paste for paper. One experiences right away the correctness of Dr. Carlton Fredericks's finding that "white bread is excellent for cleaning lamp-shades, wallpaper, suede shoes and a safe way of picking up glass."[2]

The subject of fats is more complex. The conventional attitude, as noted in Chapter Three, is that animal (saturated) fats are almost uniformly deleterious, while vegetable (poly-unsaturated) fats are almost uniformly beneficial. The truth, as it is starting to emerge from countless experiments, analyses, and statistical studies, presents a different picture. For example, an extensive, twenty-year study conducted under the auspices of the American Cancer Society showed that those who ate fairly freely of such frowned-upon foods as eggs and fried meats actually showed a slightly lower rate of heart disease and strokes than those who avoided such comestibles!

More selective studies indicate, as was noted in Chapter Two, that vegetable fats in their natural state can be of nutritional benefit in moderate amounts. But once such fats are hydrogenated or heated, they become nutritionally detri-mental. Unfortunately, most of the forms in which these fats are found in the supermarket fall into the latter categories. Margarine is a special offender, and keeping in mind its pro-nounced tendency to cause cancer in laboratory animals (see Chapter Three), it should be avoided at all costs. However, other oils, most notably wheat-germ oil, can be, and perhaps should be, eaten quite freely.

A similar division may occur in saturated fats. Meat fats seem to be potentially troublesome, although the evidence

---

[2]Keep in mind when at the supermarket, however, that most commercial varieties of whole-wheat and rye breads, while nutritionally superior to plain white, are still far from being all that they suggest. Not only may they contain sugar and other undesirable additives, but they usually contain a great deal of white flour as well. Be sure to carefully examine the labels of bread and other packaged foods you want to buy. Remember that the most abundant ingredients are usually placed first in the label listing.

on this is far from clearcut or completely convincing. Like heated and/or hydrogenated vegetable fats, they seem more dangerous from the standpoint of causing cancer rather than heart disease. Butterfat, on the other hand, may actually have an invigorating effect on health. According to Dr. Roger Williams, one of the world's great biochemists—he discovered pantothenic acid (the B vitamin) and made several discoveries concerning the effects and uses of folic acid—butterfat is used by the system to synthesize certain vitamins, most notably Vitamin B_6. It also, so he maintains, promotes the growth of favorable bacteria in the intestine. Since no study to my knowledge has ever linked butterfat directly with heart disease or cancer, butter can probably be eaten by most people in reasonable amounts with little fear of calamitous consequences. You will, however, do well to buy the unsalted variety rather than the salted.

Too many a diet that has eliminated or nearly eliminated sugar, salt, white flour, certain forms of fat, and much red meat, such as steaks, is one that has taken all joy out of eating, if not out of life itself. This, however, need not be the case at all. On the contrary, such a regimen can open up wholly new avenues of gustatory pleasure.

Many simple foods, such as lentils, beans, and the like, can be made into truly delicious delights, and in the process their nutritional benefits will be underscored rather than undermined. Adding garlic, chili peppers, and other such condiments and spices can greatly enhance flavor and appeal, provided such additions are made not helter-skelter but selectively and judicially. There are all kinds of dishes— chili con carne, hash, casseroles of one kind or another—that can easily be transformed with a little thought and care into scrumptious, nutritional bonanzas.

Snacks, too, can be created that will promote good health as well as good munching. For example, mix some unsalted peanuts, raisins, sunflower seeds, and pumpkin seeds in a bowl and pop half a handful in your mouth. You will be surprised at how tasty this highly nutritious mixture is.

And don't forget that some suspect foods have been investigated and given "a clean bill of health." Coffee, to take one well-known example, is often thought to cause a lot of medical mischief. Yet studies show this popular beverage to be less threatening to health than you may think. One extensive study of over 72,000 employees at IBM could find no correlation at all between coffee and blood pressure. Those who drank a goodly amount of coffee averaged blood pressure readings no higher than those who drank none. Another study found no relation between coffee consumption and blood cholesterol. Such studies do not suggest that one can consume cup after cup of coffee, day after day, with impunity. Excessive coffee ingestion will definitely and adversely affect the stomach, bladder, and nervous system. Some recent evidence suggests that pregnant women drinking twelve or more cups a day may tend to have children with birth defects. But apparently most people can drink, say, three or four cups a day without being notably the worse for doing so.

As for alcohol, the news concerning this beverage is not exclusively negative. Judicially used, alcohol, so it seems, will add to, not detract from, human health. This first point came to light in a scientific sense when doctors attached to a California-based health-maintenance organization (the Kaiser Permanente Plan) began noticing the high number of teetotalers among those suffering their first heart attacks. Follow-up studies only confirmed the initial finding. Those who completely abstained from alcohol were significantly more likely to suffer a heart attack than those who customarily enlivened their days with one or two drinks.

Moderate drinkers apparently have higher levels of certain blood proteins that are believed to protect the human body from heart ailments. Another factor, however, may be alcohol's long-known tendency to expand, at least temporarily, the blood vessels. Whatever the reason, the research is clear and unmistakable: Those who imbibe one or two drinks a day live in less danger of a heart attack than do those who drink less or not at all.

This should not, however, send anyone scurrying to the liquor cabinet, eager to down everything in sight with a view of making themselves healthier. People who drink more than two drinks a day have a higher heart-attack rate than total abstainers. Once again, moderation provides the key.

As with alcohol and coffee, so with almost everything else in terms of setting a healthy table. There is no need to banish any food completely from your life. Small amounts of even the most offensive junk foods can be consumed occasionally without any dire danger of damage to the human system. Good nutrition simply means adding more and more of the better foods and less and less of the bad ones to our daily diets. In this way we will add more years to our lives, and more and more life to our years, as well.

II

While food, or at any rate the right kind of food, can do much to help us live longer and livelier lives, food supplements can give an extra, and comparatively easy, boost along the way. Pill popping, providing it involves popping the right kind of pills, is something that every health-conscious person should indulge in.

Offering such a suggestion, however, opens up one of the most rankling controversies in modern medicine. The American Medical Association and the American Diabetic Association are both on record as maintaining that all the vitamins and minerals a normal person needs are available in a well-balanced diet. These organizations claim that any additional amounts obtained through supplements are superfluous and possibly even dangerous. Since these two organizations would seem to be the most authoritative in the field, how, you may be wondering, do nonphysicians such as I dare say something so radically different?

There are three basic reasons for believing that the AMA's and the ADA's long-standing position on food supplements is now totally outmoded.

The first fact is that what these organizations call a well-balanced diet will no longer furnish even those minimal amounts of nutrients which these organizations themselves admit to be necessary for human health. New forms of farming, for one thing, have altered the composition of the soils to the detriment of the crops grown in them. New chemical fertilizers, while they may not directly damage the nutritional value of the crops they fertilize, do tend to destroy certain trace minerals in the soil. And the depletion of these trace minerals does directly and distinctly affect the mineral content of the crops. For example, in 1969 the *National Hog Farmer,* an agricultural magazine, reported an alarming phenomenon: Pigs in farms throughout the country were going into convulsions and even dying. The cause, according to two scientists who had probed the matter, was that the pigs were being fed corn grown on chemically fertilized soil, and since this soil now lacked zinc, so did the corn it produced. The porkers were thus suffering, said the scientists, from a zinc deficiency.

Since that time many farmers have begun giving their pigs zinc supplements. As a matter of fact it has become customary to supplement the feed of many animals with various trace minerals of one kind or another. But human beings, according to conventional wisdom, need only a "well-balanced diet" to obtain all the nutritional factors they can possibly use. As a result, mineral and vitamin deficiencies have become widespread.

The second reason for disbelieving the AMA and ADA claims is the mounting pile of scientific evidence showing how particular vitamins and/or minerals, taken in amounts far beyond those found in any "well-balanced" diet, can prevent and sometimes cure many illnesses. Some of this evidence has already been presented in previous chapters of this book. More will be given in the bibliographic notes and comments. And more, much more, is provided in the pages of numerous and noteworthy scientific journals such as the *Journal of Clinical Nutrition, Nutrition Reviews, Clinical Engineering, Science, Scientific American*, and others. Since most of these discoveries are not reported in the standard medical journals, most doctors do not know about them. But they exist nevertheless, and their number is growing all the time.

The third reason for disagreeing with the AMA and ADA stance on food supplements is for most of us the most compelling of all: Some of the world's most distinguished physicians and scientists no longer agree with it. Among those who are on record as endorsing the taking of such food supplements as vitamin pills are the following:

- Three different winners of the Nobel Prize for medicine: Drs. Albert Szent–Gyorgyi, Hans Krebs, and Linus Pauling. (Dr. Pauling is the only person ever to win two unshared Nobel Prizes.)
- The country's most famous heart surgeon: Dr. Alton Ochsner, founder of the world-famed Ochsner Clinic in New Orleans.
- The former director of the National Cancer Institute: Dr. Arthur Upton, whose vitamin pill intake was discussed in Chapter Three.
- The world's foremost authority on stress: Dr. Hans Selye, formerly professor of medicine at McGill

University Medical School and currently president of the International Institute of Stress.

- A former chairman of the AMA's own Food and Nutrition Council: Dr. Charles Butterworth, currently professor of medicine at the University of Alabama Medical School.
- The country's most distinguished biochemist: Dr. Roger Williams, who became the first biochemist to be elected president of the American Chemical Society.
- One of the country's "top doctors": Theodore Cooper, who was Assistant Secretary for Health in the federal government's Department of Health and Human Services in the Carter Administration.

This is only a partial list, but it should be enough to convince you that if you defy conventional "wisdom" by taking food supplements such as vitamin pills, you will find yourself in some pretty good company. And if anyone you know, including your doctor, starts to sneer or make fun of you for taking such supplements, simply show him, her, or them the list and ask them if they feel their qualifications are superior to those of these "pill poppers."

But if food supplements can help mightily in building health, what food supplements and how much of them should be taken?

Let us start with vitamins: Vitamin A can be taken in amounts ranging from 5,000 units (or less) to 25,000 units a day.

Turning to Vitamin B we find a whole complex of factors—some eleven vitamins have been identified in this group. It is best to make sure you get some of each, and how much of each you will want to take will vary somewhat. Fifty milligrams a day is a good minimum goal for Vitamins B_1, B_2, B_6, inositol, choline, pantothenic acid, and para-aminobenzoic

TABLE 6
National Academy of Science's
Recommended Daily Allowances
for Vitamins & Minerals

	Infants 0–12 months		Children under 4 years		Adults & children 4 or more years		Pregnant or lactating women	
Vitamin A	1,500	IU	2,500	IU	5,000	IU	8.000	IU
Vitamin D	400	IU	400	IU	400	IU	400	IU
Vitamin E	5	IU	10	IU	15	IU	15	IU
Vitamin C	35	mg	40	mg	60	mg	60	mg
Vitamin B_1	0.5	mg	0.7	mg	1.5	mg	1.7	mg
Vitamin B_2	0.6	mg	0.8	mg	1.7	mg	2	mg
Vitamin B_3	8	mg	9	mg	20	mg	20	mg
Vitamin B_6	0.4	mg	0.7	mg	2	mg	2.5	mg
Vitamin B_{12}	2	mcg	3	mcg	6	mcg	8	mcg
Folic Acid	0.1	mg	0.2	mg	0.4	mg	0.8	mg
Biotin	0.05	mg	0.15	mg	0.3	mg	0.3	mg
Pantothenic Acid	3	mg	5	mg	10	mg	10	mg
Calcium	600	mg	800	mg	1,000	mg	1,300	mg
Magnesium	70	mg	200	mg	400	mg	450	mg
Iron	15	mg	10	mg	18	mg	18	mg
Zinc	5	mg	8	mg	15	mg	15	mg
Iodine	45	mcg	70	mcg	150	mcg	150	mcg

Note: The figures above should be considered minimum requirements only since many nutritionally oriented physicians believe that substantially larger amounts of most of them (iron is an exception) are needed to ensure maximum health. Phosphorus and copper have been omitted from the list since the average American diet usually provides ample amounts of these two minerals.

acid. For folic acid, biotin, and B_{12}, smaller quantities can be consumed. B-complex vitamin tablets that provide 50 milligrams of the first seven B factors usually provide 100 micrograms (one-tenth of a milligram) of folic acid and 50 micrograms each of biotin and B_{12}.

Vitamin C can be taken in amounts ranging from 500 to 5,000 milligrams or more daily. Linus Pauling takes 10,000 milligrams per day while Dr. Fred Klenner, a physician in North Carolina who has been working with Vitamin C since the 1940s, takes 18,000 milligrams daily. Now approaching eighty years of age, Dr. Klenner remains remarkably alert and vigorous. For that matter, so does Dr. Albert Szent–Gyorgyi, the physician who won the Nobel Prize for discovering Vitamin C almost fifty years ago and who has taken well over 2,000 milligrams of it every day since. Now eighty-eight years old, he still works daily at his laboratory in Woods Hole, Massachusetts.

A health-conscious person will also want to take from 400 to 4,000 units of Vitamin D and from 200 to 1,200 units of Vitamin E. This will complete your vitamin-enrichment program.

Turning to minerals, the first to consider are calcium and magnesium. These two vital nutrients should be taken together since they are mutually dependent in a sense, and an increase in one should be balanced with an increase in the other. However, they need not and perhaps should not be taken in equal quantities, for the body needs more calcium than magnesium. Unless you are getting a good deal of calcium in your regular diet, it is best to take at least twice as much calcium as magnesium. Dolomite, a natural substance from the Dolomite Mountains in Italy, which is sold in health-food stores, provides calcium and magnesium in a two-to-one ratio. Three or four tablets will yield 180 to 240 milligrams of magnesium and 360 to 480 milligrams of calcium. For additional calcium, bone-meal tablets are recommended.

Zinc is the only other mineral for which supplements are normally needed. Anywhere from 10 to 100 milligrams per day can be of benefit. Ample amounts of potassium, chromium, selenium, and other important minerals can usually be obtained totally through proper diet, but anyone wishing to take additional amounts can obtain safe supplements of most of these minerals in health-food stores and some drug stores. Kelp tablets, derived from seaweed, contain many valuable minerals, including iodine.

You will have noticed that ranges rather than specific quantities have been recommended. In deciding just how much you want to take, you should take into account such factors as age, weight, and physical condition. Larger people need more nutrients than smaller people. Older people generally require more than younger ones since the body assimilates and utilizes vitamins less efficiently as it ages. Thus greater supplies are necessary to do the work which lesser amounts accomplished in the past. And the poorer one's physical condition is, the more supplementation it may take to make a significant difference.

Is there any danger, you may be wondering, of taking too much? Not really, as long as you stay within the recommended dosages. Vitamin C, being an acid, does create some heartburn in a few people, but even they can usually get around this by taking the vitamin with some bland foods that can act as an acid buffer. Otherwise, the vitamin seems to offer little danger. In the near half-century of its use, there has never been a single case of someone causing themselves any serious harm from taking too much Vitamin C. When the body has had all the Vitamin C it can handle, it starts to develop diarrhea, and some physicians who work with the vitamin say this "diarrhea index" serves as a valuable signal of when to stop taking any more.[3]

None of the B vitamins has ever been found to foster any maladies, and many "health nuts" consume several times the amount recommended above. I myself take double the

[3]Vitamin C does, however, change the composition of the urine in such a way as to make a lab technician sometimes suspect that the person taking it has diabetes. If you are taking a lot of Vitamin C and are being tested for diabetes, inform those who are doing the test about your Vitamin-C intake. Or, to be sure of preventing any mistake in the lab analysis, simply stop taking the vitamin a few days before the test.

dosages I have recommended, which were designed more as minimum than maximum suggestions. The same holds true for Vitamin E with one exception: This vitamin, when taken in high dosages, does tend to elevate the blood pressure temporarily in some people who have elevated blood pressure. The effect is only temporary and occurs only in some hypertensive people, but to be on the safe side if you have high blood pressure, start by taking only 30 or so units per day for one week, gradually increasing the amount each week. Handled in this way, it should cause no harm.

Vitamins A and D have been known to cause problems when ingested in large amounts over extended periods of time. But such cases are quite rare and have involved mostly children. Keeping within the guidelines suggested above should present no problems to anyone.

It is interesting to observe in this connection that Eskimos living in their native environment and eating their traditional foods consume close to 300,000 units of Vitamin A daily! Furthermore, their intake of Vitamin D surpasses by far the supposedly "safe" level, yet no Eskimo has ever been known to have suffered from hypervitaminosis, the medical term used to describe an illness caused by excessive vitamin intake.

One can, of course, argue that Eskimos through the years have built up an exceptionally high tolerance for such vitamins. Yet in modern society we have the case of the physician, George Whipple, who won the Nobel Prize for finding out that liver, thanks to its high iron content, could cure anemia. Liver is also an extraordinarily rich source of Vitamin A, and many of Whipple's patients thus ended up ingesting over 100,000 units of this vitamin every day over a span of many years. At this level of intake, Vitamin A is considered medically harmful. Yet no case of hypervitaminosis was ever reported from among his patients.

The answer to this puzzling paradox may lie in the fact

that Whipple's patients, like the traditional Eskimos, were getting their Vitamin A in its natural form, and in this form even otherwise excessive levels of the vitamins may not do any damage. In any event, those taking Vitamin A might do well to buy tablets that are made from a natural source, such as cod-liver oil or some other fish-liver oil. In this form these tablets will also contain Vitamin D, and in this form neither should pose any problem, even if your intake should exceed the recommended amounts.

What about other vitamins? Should they also be taken only in their natural form or, to put it more explicitly, in a form derived from natural sources?

This question has generated a good deal of discussion and debate in the health field in recent years. Many experts claim that a vitamin is a vitamin and it doesn't make a bit of difference whether it is synthetically created or naturally derived. But others cite a small yet not insignificant body of evidence indicating that a meaningful difference exists in terms of effects. Vitamin C, for example, in its natural form is accompanied by substances called bioflavonoids, and according to some scientists, these bioflavonoids benefit the smaller blood vessels.

So what should one do? Some, like me, compromise. I take Vitamins A and D that are naturally derived from fish-liver oils. I take some naturally derived Vitamin C and let synthetic preparations supply the rest of my intake. And I take mostly synthetic Vitamins B and E, although I occasionally substitute some of the natural Vitamin E for whatever added benefit, if any, it may bestow.

The reason for not taking naturally derived vitamins exclusively is to save money, for the synthetically created ones are much cheaper. Fortunately the cost of vitamin and mineral supplementation lies well within the reach of most people, including even those who have to budget carefully. And with the savings to be made by following the dietary recommendations made earlier, such as substituting beans and cereals for steaks and chops, many should have enough left over from their food shopping to finance their food supplements as well.

So far the discussion of food and food supplements has centered almost exclusively on the needs of adults, but obviously children can benefit greatly from the dietary measures which have been discussed. They too need less sugar and salt in their diets and more fruits, vegetables, and whole grains. Probably one of the greatest health crimes of our times is the way so many harmful foods—foods that are filled with sugar and/or salt, white flour, and chemicals—are looked upon and utilized as "children's foods." Children can also greatly benefit from food supplements with the dosages reduced somewhat to allow for their smaller size.

III

But food and food supplements do not offer the only keys to good health. Physical activity may be just as important. We have seen the role it can play in preventing or controlling such all-too-common black illnesses as high blood pressure and diabetes. Cancer too may be curbed through exercise, for laboratory experiments show that test animals that are exercised regularly acquire increased resistance to cancer-causing chemicals. In short, physical activity must be a crucial component of any healthy person's lifestyle.

But this does not mean that you have to rush out to sign up for tennis lessons or for a golf-club membership. You don't even need a pair of running shoes. As pointed out in Chapter Two, such forms of exercise might not be the most effective and might even be harmful for some people. The most beneficial forms of physical activity are balanced, rhythmic, and only mildly competitive.

Balanced exercise does not stress or develop some

parts of the body more than others. Rhythmic exercise is characterized for the most part by a steady, continuous motion, not by starts and stops. And all competitive exercise is not relegated to playing opposite a partner or partners: The jogger who sets excessive goals for himself/herself and then strains to reach them is engaged in a highly competitive exercise.

Dancing, swimming, and cross-country skiing are among the best examples of sports that meet these three suggested standards. But do not neglect the simplest and easiest one of all—walking. It requires no special equipment, no special time, and no special place—and several studies indicate that it may produce results as good as if not better than that of any other form of physical activity.

Try to build more walking into your daily routine. For example, if you drive to work, try parking your car further away and walking the rest of the way. If you take public transportation, get off a station or two earlier and walk.

Do not neglect stairs because climbing them can be the most effective walking exercise of all. Here again you should try to incorporate the activity into your everyday living pattern. If you work in an office on the tenth floor, try walking up to the second or third floor and taking the elevator from there. Remember that the two geographical areas where people frequently live well beyond one hundred years of age—a district in Southern Russia and a region in Pakistan—are both nestled within mountains, and their healthy residents spend much of their time climbing up and down slopes. In this country, the community which for many years enjoyed the lowest heart attack rate in the United States was Roseta, Pennsylvania. The small town's general store and post office were located on top of a hill, thus requiring most of its residents to climb up and down every day.

Another option for improving health is available to

women and not to men. This is breast feeding. A landmark study carried out some years ago showed that mothers who breast feed their children develop a remarkable resistance to breast cancer. Indeed, the indications are that if a woman breast feeds enough—two children for six months each seems to be the minimum—she will develop a virtual immunity to this major form of malignancy.

Breast feeding, it should be further noted, also yields benefits for the child. Mother's milk contains much more Vitamin E, magnesium, and other valuable nutrients than does cow's milk, especially true when the latter has been pasteurized as it almost invariably has. Its fat/protein ratio is different, and it contains other substances which improve the infant's immune system. Finally, breast feeding creates ties of tenderness between mother and child which protect and promote the emotional well-being of both.

Attitude may well be the most critical factor of all in fostering health. In a very real sense, health is a state of mind as much as a state of body. People who go toward life with a positive attitude will, on the average, suffer less illness and live longer. A healthy involvement in life itself is a health builder *par excellence*.

A bit of irony here is that people who are overly concerned about their health can end up with less health rather than more because a preoccupation with one's own personal well-being is far from healthy. Part of the proper attitude involves caring about and working for people or things outside of oneself. The Bible intimates that those who put their personal desires aside may end up with more, not less, to show for it. There is a lot of evidence to indicate that, in terms of health at least, such gains are to be realized. Virtue is its own reward, said the ancients, and if we count better health as a reward, the ancients knew what they were talking about.

IV

As pointed out in Chapter One, the 1960s and 1970s saw the development of several programs which should have greatly reduced the discrepancy between the health of blacks and that of whites: the food-stamp program, the expansion of school lunch programs, the start-up of school breakfasts in some areas, and, most of all, Medicare and Medicaid, which gave the country's black population much greater access to medical care.

The increase in medical care was especially dramatic. By the end of the 1970s, blacks were visiting the doctor almost as frequently as whites. And when one bears in mind the fact that the black population as a group is appreciably younger than the white population, the number of physician visits perhaps more than balances out.

But what has been the effect of this increased health care on black health? Again, referring back to Chapter One, it will be recalled that during this era black longevity did increase slightly more than white longevity. There was, therefore, some slight decline in the relative difference between the races in this regard. But it will also be recalled that this relative gain by blacks was more than accounted for by the remarkable rise in the rate of white homicide victims. When this was factored out, we saw that the gap between the two races in terms of illness-caused death and disability actually increased while the gap in their relative access to medical care was substantially reduced. To put it still more succinctly, a *relative increase in health care for black Americans produced a relative decrease in their health.*

That more health care has not led to more health for the country's black population does not necessarily imply by any means that they have been singled out or victimized in any special way. Rather, it indicates that the nation's health-care system is suffering from some very real sicknesses of its own.

A lot of data have emerged in recent years to show that this is indeed the case. For example, Dr. Michael Miller, a sociologist at the University of Arkansas, found that those areas which have the most doctors also have the highest death rates. This is especially true if a high percentage of the doctors are surgeons.[4]

The figures on what happens to death rates when doctors go on strike underscore Dr. Miller's research. Such strikes do not happen frequently, but they do on occasion occur, and the results that occur when they do take place should give any reasonable human being considerable cause for concern.

During the 1970s, there were three notable strikes by physicians. One was in Bogotá, Colombia, one was in Israel, and one was in California. In all three instances, emergency care was provided but all other medical services were withheld. As a consequence, the number of operations performed in California during the period of the strike dropped by two-thirds, while in Israel the number of physician–patient contacts declined by over 80 percent.

What were the results? The number of deaths dropped dramatically in all three situations, declining by 35 percent in Bogotá, 50 percent in Israel, and 18 percent in California. In all three places, the death rates returned to their former levels once the physicians went back to full-time practice.

These figures indicate that much of the "health care" being provided by modern medicine may be making people less healthy rather than more. And if this inference still seems irresponsible and irrational, then there is plenty of more detailed data to back it up and explain it. One study of a Maryland hospital found that one-quarter of its patients were admitted suffering from the side effects of prescription drugs.

---

[4]He also found, interestingly, that the presence of nurses had the opposite effect. Those areas with the most nurses tended to have lower rates of mortality.

Other figures demonstrate that when surgeons are paid for each operation they perform, they perform tens of thousands of unnecessary operations leading to at least 12,000 deaths a year in this country alone. And even the *Journal of the American Medical Association* has admitted that physician-administered injections of estrogen and DES have led to increased cancer among women.

Many doctors have spoken out against this depressing state of affairs. Says Dr. Bernard Rimland, a San Diego pediatrician, "Modern medicine is bankrupt. It's becoming a nightmare. The advances have backfired leaving in their wake death, blindness, stroke and a variety of other iatrogenic [physician caused] disasters more serious than the original disease. The side effects of prescription drugs now equal breast cancer as a leading cause of death in the United States." Comments Dr. Mark Altshule of Harvard's prestigious medical school, "Modern medicine is based largely on superstition."

It is important to note that the orientation of modern medicine affects the rich as well as the poor. What happened to Aristotle Onassis is a case in point. In the opinion of one Long Island physician, Dr. Hosein Ghadimi, "One of the richest men in the world died of starvation. Aristotle Onassis had myasthenia gravis and couldn't chew . . . they gave him intravenous glucose. Patients on such a miserable diet die from malnutrition." A still more recent example is the Shah of Iran. One of the most elaborate and expensive medical teams ever assembled gave him chemotherapy for his cancer. However, the chemotherapy destroyed his immune system, and this in turn caused him to contract other ailments which led to his death.

The lesson from all this is a simple, stark, and very important one. The key to improving black health does not for the most part lie in making available more medical services to more black people. Though there are situations where more medical services would be helpful, the real keys to enhancing black health lie elsewhere. They lie in changing the country's medical system into what it purports to be but what at present it so obviously and so tragically isn't: a genuine health-care system.

The task seems tremendous but it can be done, and indeed, slowly, very slowly, it is being done. The nub of the problem is probably the reward system. As we saw in Chapter One, change would probably cause the "health-care system" to go bankrupt. What we need is to change this completely around so that the system and those who labor within it would actually get richer by promoting health.

One of the most hopeful devices for moving toward this goal is the health-maintenance organization (HMO). Such an organization agrees to take care of all of a person's medical needs for a flat monthly or yearly fee, which may be paid by the government, the individual's employer, or the individual himself/herself. Under such a plan, the HMO has an incentive for keeping its patients healthy, for the healthier they are, the less cost and more profit for the HMO.

The HMOs already in existence have demonstrated some ability to cut costs and improve health. For example, their clients average only about one-half as much in the hospital as do those whose medical insurance offers payment for each service performed, including each day spent in the hospital. The HMOs would be even more successful, however, if their physicians did not suffer from the same faulty training that physicians suffer from generally in the country, namely training that stresses drugs, surgery, and supposedly curative approaches while neglecting nutrition, lifestyle adjustment, and preventive approaches. Nevertheless, they do signal a valuable start in the right direction.

The fight for a healthier Black America should also spread to parts other than just that of the medical system. Blacks should seek improvements in school lunch and breakfast programs, which today consist all too frequently of nutritionally inferior foods. They should seek even more general health-producing reforms, such as federal requirements for increased enrichment, including increased fiber, in flour and bread, better labeling of the salt and sugar added to canned foods, and possibly even heavy taxes on such injurious foods as candy to discourage their consumption. We already tax cigarettes and liquor in this fashion, so why cannot we extend the same policy to other noxious substances?

Blacks and black organizations should also give careful consideration to whether or not they want to continue supporting the federal government's food-stamp program. A University of Virginia economist who analyzed Department of Agriculture statistics regarding the program's impact on the nutritional level of its participants came to the conclusion that the stamps were worsening the health of those who received them. This was because too many of the recipients were using the stamps to buy more sweets and fatty foods. The former program under which the federal government distributed simple but generally nutritious foods directly to the needy may have served the cause of black health better.

But, you may now be saying, all the recommendations you have been making for social action to improve black health are general policy recommendations which are likely to improve white health as well. That is true, for while efforts to increase the supply of black physicians and, in some areas, the supply of medical services available to blacks certainly need to continue, they will not make any important improvements in the overall health of Black America unless and until more general and more fundamental alterations are made in American health policy. This means that the fight for a healthier Black America is part and parcel of the fight for a healthier overall America, period. When it comes to health, blacks and whites share a common battle and a common goal, and neither can go forward without helping the other. This commonality of purpose and pursuit should produce some valuable side effects in terms of increased amity and mutual respect between the races as both struggle to transform the American health-care system into one that will genuinely provide and promote better health for one and for all.

Chapter Eight

Late Developments

There is always a necessary interval between the time a book is completed and the time it goes into production. The interval in the case of this book saw several new developments come to light in the quickly developing field of black health.

First and foremost were the latest figures on black cancer, which the National Cancer Institute released in November 1980. They made for grim reading. Cancer among both blacks and whites had risen rapidly during the previous quarter century, but the increase for blacks had been at an 8 percent higher rate than that for whites. More significantly, the death rate from cancer had shot up 25 percent faster than it had for whites. In other words, not only was cancer increasing faster among blacks, but blacks' survival rate, as compared to whites', was falling increasingly behind. While 41 percent of all whites who contracted cancer could expect to be alive in five years, only 30 percent of all cancer-afflicted blacks could expect to live that long. (A person who is still alive five years after the disease strikes is considered cured.)

Especially affected by this unwelcome turn of events were black males. In 1915 they placed at the bottom of the list of those likely to die of cancer. Black females were then the most frequent fatalities of the disease. They were followed by white females and white males. But by the start of the 1980s, black males had jumped to the top of the list while black females held second place.

Some statistics on specific cancers spell out the dimensions of this discrepancy between the races. More than two-fifths of all white males who contract rectal cancer will end up "cured," but less than one-fifth of all black males will be so fortunate. And while over two-thirds of all white women suffering from breast cancer survive the disease, less than half of all black women victims do.

Two reasons have been advanced to help explain this dramatic difference in cancer survival. First, blacks are more likely to wait longer before getting their illnesses diagnosed. As Dr. Laselle D. Laffall, chairman of surgery at the Howard University Medical School put it, "The biggest problem is that there are many people who believe that cancer can't be cured—period. They have to be motivated to seek care . . ." (The Boston Globe, October 26, 1980).

The second reason given for the lower survival rate is that blacks are less likely to receive the more intensive and up-to-date medical care once their cancer has been diagnosed. The reduced economic resources of most blacks place the services of the leading cancer specialists beyond their reach, although, as pointed out earlier, it is not certain how much of a difference the most intensive cancer therapy makes when it comes to curing the disease.

Aside from these factors, it seems most likely that changes in the black lifestyle undoubtedly contribute to this trend. Sugar, salt, fats, and beef have become a much greater part of the black diet in recent years, and we have already seen the part such dietary factors can play in cancer. Drinking and cigarette smoking must also be considered. The incidence of cigarette smoking among blacks is 10 percent greater than among whites, and some doctors believe that cigarettes not only cause 90 percent of all lung cancers but contribute to the development of some other kinds of cancer as well.

When it comes to sickle-cell anemia, the news is far more encouraging. First, further evidence has emerged spotlighting the value of Vitamin E in combating this rather mysterious malady. In May 1980, the *American Journal of Clinical Nutrition* published research results showing that an intake of 150 units of Vitamin E three times a day, 450 units in all, would reduce the number of irreversibly sickled cells by about one-half. And on June 9, 1980, *Medical World News* reported a preliminary study at Harvard University which showed that a salt-free diet could greatly reduce both the frequency and severity of sickle-cell crisis. Then, early in 1981 the United States Air Force Academy abolished its policy of refusing to accept as cadets blacks who were carriers of the sickle-cell trait.

In regard to the continuing, and even widening, gap between white and black infant death rates, recent research focuses on a new factor in the situation—the difference in birth weights. A black child, so studies now show, is more than twice as likely as a white child to be born underweight. According to a report in the *New York Times* on December 28, 1980, this difference "accounted almost entirely for the unhappy fact that a black infant was twice as likely to die within four weeks" as a white infant. The newspaper went on to point out that "two-thirds of all babies who die are of low weight."

Here again the greater incidence of smoking among blacks appears to be a contributing factor, for studies have long demonstrated that mothers who smoke tend to have smaller babies. But inadequate prenatal care, faulty nutrition, and other factors cannot be excluded.

Finally, there is one group of ailments, not covered in the text, which also affect blacks as much, if not more, than whites. These are back problems. In this connection it might be useful to call attention to the help that chiropractors can often provide.

Chiropractors are not doctors. They cannot perform surgery or prescribe drugs. But they are trained to manipulate the spine, and they can sometimes work wonders when it comes to alleviating back pain. It is certainly too bad that so few black people seek them out. It is also unfortunate that there are almost no black chiropractors.

There are substantial differences in degrees of skill and even integrity among chiropractors, as there are among doctors, and so you should use care in selecting one. The best way, perhaps, is simply to ask around until you find one who appears to have a good track record. In the meantime, do not neglect the basic methods for protecting your back. These include standing up straight, not slouching on overstuffed chairs and sofas, and sleeping on a firm, even mattress. Also, always bend your knees when bending over. These are simple rules to follow, and, as this book seeks to demonstrate, following simple rules is essentially what good health is all about.

Annotated
Bibliography

CHAPTER ONE
BLACK HEALTH: CRISIS AND CROSSROADS

Nearly all the figures on black health in this chapter are taken from *Health, United States, 1979,* a publication of the United States Department of Health, Education and Welfare (now called the Department of Health and Human Services). Some additional figures are available in "On the Health of Black Americans" by Therman E. Evans, M.D., in *Ebony,* March 1977. Dr. Evans's figures are more detailed in some respects but are less up to date than those used in the HEW report since his article was written and published before the HEW report was prepared. The quote from Dr. Evans on the role of nutrition in health, used later in this chapter, was also taken from his *Ebony* article.

A United Press International dispatch on Charlie Smith appeared in many newspapers on October 7, 1979.

Shortly after his death, *The New York Times* published its piece on centenarians on December 9, 1979.

Dr. Michael Lathem, who designed the questionnaire used by the *National Enquirer,* is quoted by *Time* in its December 18, 1972, issue as saying, "Nine out of ten doctors in New York City would give wrong answers to dietary questions." The survey at the Harvard Medical School was reported by Dr. Jean Meyer on a local (Boston) television show in the mid-seventies. Dr. Meyer is presently president of Tufts University. If the reader is further unconvinced of the nutritional ignorance of most doctors, then he or she should examine a copy of the March 7, 1980, issue of the *Journal of the American Medical Association.* The issue carries the association's annual report on Medical Education in the United States. In the issue's 145 pages, which list all the subjects being taught at the nation's medical schools, the word "nutrition" does not appear even once!

The data on eggs and their lack of effect in increasing cholesterol is fairly voluminous. To cite just one example, the *Journal of the American Medical Association* on October 25, 1976, reported an intensive dietary study of a ten-thousand-member community—Tecumseh, Michigan. The doctors from the University of Michigan Medical School who carried out the study confessed that they could find no relationship at all between the amount of cholesterol in a person's diet and the amount of cholesterol in that person's blood. Much of this debunking research is summarized in a short monograph by Mark Altshule, M.D., entitled "On the Much Maligned Egg," *Executive Health,* Vol. X, No. 8, 1974. For an interesting piece written by two data analysts with no particular knowledge of nutrition but with an awareness of how figures can be finagled, see "Egg in Your Bier?" in the Winter 1980 issue of *The Public Interest.*

CHAPTER TWO
THE NUMBER-ONE KILLER

For some of the basic data on high blood pressure I am indebted to Carlson Wade and his useful book *Hypertension (High Blood Pressure) and Your Diet* (New Canaan: Keats Publishing, 1975). The figures on hypertension among blacks, however, come from *Health, United States, 1979,* the HEW report cited in Chapter One. The Northwestern University study which showed that hypertensive people contract cancer more frequently than those whose blood pressure is normal is cited in Frank Murray's *Program Your Heart For Health* (New York: Larchmont, 1977). This easy-to-read and most informative work is highly recommended to all those who want to know more about heart health. (And that should include just about everyone.)

For material on how smoking elevates blood pressure, see either the book cited above by Murray or almost any general book on hypertension and/or heart disease. The rules and procedures for practicing meditation are based on my own experience for I took instruction in the technique in the early 1970s and have been meditating faithfully twice a day since. Probably the best all-around book on the subject is *The Relaxation Response* by Herbert Benson, M.D. (New York: William Morrow, 1975). In this brief but valuable work, Dr. Benson describes the results of his own tests on meditation and details the methods by which everyone can take advantage of what the simple practice has to offer.

For further information on the role which various foods can play in either stimulating or sedating your appetite for tobacco, see "A Diet to Help You Quit Smoking" in *Prevention* magazine, October 1979.

The Israeli weight-loss/blood-pressure-reduction experiment was reported in the January 8, 1978, *New York Times.* For figures on black obesity, see "Obesity: A Deadly

Burden" in *Essence*, June 1980. For more detailed data on this subject see Mitchell *et al.*, *Nutrition in Health and Science* (Philadelphia: Lippincott, 1976). The quote from Dr. Barbara Edelstein is from her book *The Woman Doctor's Diet for Women* (Englewood Cliffs, N.J.: Prentice-Hall, Inc., 1976).

Perhaps the best article on the way high-fiber consumption can lead to weight loss appeared in the *Lancet* of December 22, 1973. The writer, Dr. K. W. Heaton of the British Royal Infirmary, not only reported some of the results of experiments in this vein but also discussed just how the results occurred. Dr. Hans Kaunitz of the Columbia University College of Physicians and Surgeons found that overweight patients would not only lose pounds on a high-fiber diet but would not regain them as long as they continued to consume fibrous foods.

Dr. Altshule's remarks on the importance of dividing up food intake into many meals appear in his book *Nutri tional Factors in General Medicine* (Springfield, Ill.: Charles C Thomas, 1978). Another physician who has written on this point is Dr. Josef B. Hrachovec. An expert on aging who has conducted research on this subject at the University of California, Dr. Hrachovec says several small meals are better than fewer, larger ones for "an unusually high level of triglycerides and glucose in the blood can cause a traffic jam: more fuel is being dumped into the blood stream than can be unloaded and used in the tissue cells." The result, says Dr. Hrachovec in his book *Keeping Young and Living Longer* (Los Angeles: Sherbourne, 1972), is a stored-up surplus which we call fat.

Dr. Williams's remark on the relationship between exercise and appetite control appears in his outstanding work *Nutrition Against Disease*, which is currently available in a paperback edition put out by Bantam. I urge everyone interested in health to put this book near or at the top of their reading lists. And do not neglect the notes at the rear of the book for they contain reams of intriguing and informative material.

Dr. Phillips's comments on eating and interpersonal relationships can be found in *Ebony*, January 1978. They appear on page 32 in an interesting article on obesity.

Some further tips on losing weight: Drink several glasses of water or some other unsugared liquid every day and start dinner and/or lunch with hot soup. The liquid will help give you a filled-up feeling while the soup will require you to eat slowly. However, some nutritionists claim that people who drink a lot of water tend to wash many minerals and at least some vitamins out of their system. So be sure your daily supply of nutrients is more than ample if you decide to seriously increase your water intake.

The study of 2,000 blacks and whites which confirmed the ability of potassium to counteract, at least to some degree, the effects of sodium in raising blood pressure was carried out by the Johns Hopkins School of Hygiene and Public Health. An account of its findings can be found in *Medical World News*, December 11, 1978. The results of this study, along with the one cited from Jackson, Mississippi, and others all showing the same thing (that is, the part potassium can play in reducing blood pressure) are available in an article entitled "Potassium—A Natural High Blood Pressure Preventive," in *Prevention*, November 1978.

The Louisiana study on the way black and white children handle sodium is reported in the *New York Times*, November 28, 1978. Dr. Hugh C. Trowell's stimulating monograph, "A New Dietary Explanation for the Cause of Essential Hypertension . . . the Dramatic and Significant African Experience (1929–1958)," was published by *Executive Health*, Vol. XVI, No. 2. Dr. Lemeh's statement appeared in *Ebony* in the previously cited January 1978 article.

Dr. Schroeder's best-known and landmark work is *The Trace Elements and Man* (New York: Devin–Adair, 1973).

And Dr. Pfeiffer has written at least two books, one of which has recently become available in paperback—*Zinc and Other Micro-Nutrients* (New Canaan, Ct.: Keats, 1978). Also see his monograph for *Executive Health* (Vol. XVI, No. 1) in which he sums up much of his own and Dr. Schroeder's work in this quickly developing field.

For a summary of garlic's many health-promoting qualities, including its capacity to reduce blood pressure, see the chapter on this plant in *Health Foods* by Ruth Adams and Frank Murray (New York: Larchmont, 1975). This writing team has produced a slew of valuable and readable books on health, of which this is one of the most useful to the neophyte "health nut." For later garlic research developments, which for the most part only confirm earlier findings, see *Medical Tribune*, December 6, 1978, the *American Journal of Clinical Nutrition*, September 1978, and *Atherosclerosis*, Vol. 29, 1978.

The Mormon/Seventh-Day-Adventist study was reported in *Preventive Medicine*, March 1979. The *American Journal of Epidemiology* carried a report by a Harvard research team on how they found a distinct relationship between lower blood pressure and vegetarianism. And it was the December 15, 1979, issue of the *British Medical Journal* which reported the study on high fiber and low blood pressure. An American study published in the July 1978 *American Journal of Clinical Nutrition* adds further weight to this finding.

The experiment on exposing monkeys to the stresses of ordinary human living was reported in a host of popular medical journals. See, for example, the *National Medical Bulletin* for March 6, 1979. The woman who got high blood pressure from having too many houses is reported by Adelle Davis in *Let's Get Well* (New York: Harcourt, Brace, Jovanovich, 1965). For more material on Transcendental Meditation see, besides the Benson book cited earlier, "The Physiology of

Meditation" by Robert Keith Wallance and Herbert Benson in the February 1972 *Scientific American* or the "Personal Business" section of *Business Week*, October 26, 1974. Dr. Phillips's comment on TM appears in the previously cited January 1978 article in *Ebony*.

The Michigan study linking hypertension with darkness of skin was reported in the *New York Times* on February 4, 1979. The quotation on exercise and blood pressure is from *Exercise and Coronary Heart Disease* by Gerald F. Fletcher, M.D., and John D. Cantwell, M.D. (Springfield, Ill.: Charles C Thomas, 1974). And the New York Infirmary exercise was first reported in the *Journal of the American Geriatrics Society* (Vol. 19, No. 12, 1971). A later write-up appeared in *Prevention*, May 1978.

CHAPTER THREE
CANCER

The most up-to-date figures on black cancer rates that I could find when this text was written were those from *Health, United States, 1979*, which I used in Chapter One. However, this HEW report only gives the overall black cancer rate plus the rates for the two leading cancer killers—lung and colon–rectum cancer. For a more detailed look at cancer and its relation to the Afro–American community, I had to resort to some 1969 figures which I found in a most informative article entitled "Cancers that Affect Blacks the Most" by Michele Burgen. It was published in the April 1978 issue of *Ebony*. The quotation from Dr. Leffall is taken from this same article.

Dr. Upton's statement on his personal regimen for preventing cancer appeared in the *Medical Tribune* of November 22, 1978. I have been continually amazed that no medical reporter for the conventional press has seized on this statement and given it the publicity it seems to deserve in view of

Upton's standing and in view of the great fear which so many people have of this disease.

A report on Dr. Berg's paper can be found in the *New York Times*, December 3, 1975. On October 18 of the previous year, the same newspaper carried a similar story in reporting on the near simultaneous mastectomies of Mrs. Gerald Ford and Mrs. Nelson Rockefeller. This latter article made some comparisons between Japan and the United States to back up the case against fat as a causative agent in cancer.

The University of Nebraska experiment was reported in *Nutrition Today*, January 1972, and in *Critical Reviews in Food Technology*, September 1972. For the Boston University study on fats and cancer, see the *Boston Globe*, May 12, 1977.

Dr. Burkitt's observations on fiber and cancer first appeared in this country in the *Medical World News* of January 29, 1971, in a story covering a speech he had recently made at a conference on cancer. His theories have been repeated in numerous health periodicals and books since then as evidence has accumulated to support his suppositions. In 1979 Dr. Burkitt published a book of his own for laypeople, entitled *Eat Right—To Stay Healthy and Enjoy Life More* (New York: Arco). Health professionals will also wish to consult a previous book which he edited with Dr. Hugh C. Trowel, *Refined Carbohydrate Foods and Disease* (New York: Academic Press, 1975).

Regarding certain vegetables and cancer inhibition, the University of Texas study can be read about in the *American Journal of Epidemiology*, January 1979, while the VA team's observations appeared in the February 1980 issue of *Cancer Research*. The reference for the National Cancer Institute's early study on Vitamin C as a cancer inhibitor is *Oncology*, Vol. 23, 1969, pp. 33–43. It is not only amazing but also appalling that the orthodox medical world has simply ignored it. Orthodox medicine has also sought to shut its eyes regarding the still more sensational experiment carried out in

Scotland. A full account of it appeared in the October 1976 *Proceedings of the National Academy of Sciences.* A shorter account appeared in *Executive Health,* Vol. XVI, No. 4, January 1980, as well as in some popular but unconventional health magazines. Most medical journals, however, seem to have erected a wall of silence around this study.

Sister/Dr. Poydock's Vitamin C/B_{12} experiments were recounted in *Experimental Cell Biology,* Vol. 47, 1979. The *New England Journal of Medicine* of September 27, 1979, carried the report of the Mayo clinic experiment, and although the article did say in passing that chemotherapy might have prevented any beneficial effects from Vitamin C, it made no attempt to prevent medical reporters from overlooking this casual disclaimer and from erroneously publicizing the report as proof that Vitamin C is totally valueless in fighting cancer. For a report on how the Japanese hospital is using Vitamin C, see the *Journal of the International Academy of Preventive Medicine,* Vol. 1, No. 1, 1978.

The landmark study linking garlic with cancer prevention in test animals appeared in the November 24, 1957, issue of *Science* magazine. The March–April 1958 issue of *Problems of Oncology* reported a Russian experiment on humans in which garlic was found to be effective in alleviating precancerous white spots on the lips. As for honey, the New England beekeepers study was disclosed by D. C. Jarvis, M.D., in his book *Folk Medicine* (New York: Holt, Rhinehart & Winston, 1958), while the systematic French survey is cited in *Gagnez 20 Ans de Vie Grace Aux Abeilles* by Alin Caillas (Paris: Edition de la Pensée Moderne, 1971). Although the title is somewhat sensational—it means "gain twenty more years of life thanks to the bees"—the book's author is one of France's foremost agricultural scientists.

The two articles on sugar and cancer appeared in the June 1978 *British Journal of Cancer* and the Spring 1979 issue of *Nutrition and Cancer,* while it was the July 20, 1979, issue of the *Journal of the American Medical Association* which indicted estrogen. For material on the harmfulness of tranquilizers, see a United Press International report from the Food and Drug Administration which was published in many newspapers on or around July 10, 1980. The quote from *Essence* comes from an article entitled "Eating Away at Stress," which appeared in the September 1979 issue of the magazine.

CHAPTER FOUR
DIABETES

There have been several articles in the popular press in recent years calling attention to the growing incidence of diabetes and pointing out its many signs and symptoms as well as warning of its consequences. Two articles which are quite informative on these general issues are "Battling Diabetes," which appeared in *Newsweek*, December 10, 1979, and "Diagnosis Diabetes," which was published by *Reader's Digest* in January 1976. Needless to say, the American Diabetes Association puts out numerous pamphlets and other printed material covering these points. The quotations from Dr. Atkins are from an interview with him that was published in the health magazine *Let's Live*, December 1978.

The figures on diabetes among blacks, along with the quotation from Dr. Henry, came from an article on the subject in *Ebony*, March 1979. For the source of the material on the Pima Indians, see the *New York Times* and possibly other newspapers of May 2, 1973, reporting on the testimony of Dr. George D. Campbell before the Senate Committee on Nutrition Needs. Dr. Campbell told a story at the hearing of how Dr. Burkitt, the English physician cited earlier, was amazed when, on a visit to Philadelphia, he examined some black residents of that city and found that amputations brought on by diabetic gangrene were the second most prevalent form of surgery performed on them. The Africans he had worked with in Africa had hardly ever heard of the ailment.

Dr. Rieser's findings on sugar intake and its relationship to diabetes were published in the January 1978 issue of the *American Journal of Clinical Nutrition*. The statement by Dr. Raiford is from an interview with him that was published in *Prevention*, October 1978. The issue of *Consumer Reports* alluded to was the one for March 1978. For more material on honey, see Adams and Murray, *Health Foods*, cited earlier.

In addition to the article by Dr. Trowell cited in the text, the interested reader may wish to consult the book he coedited with Dr. Burkitt, *Refined Carbohydrate Foods and Disease*, cited earlier. Dr. Burkitt's article for *Executive Health* (Vol. XVI, No. 3) entitled "Is Dietary Fibre Protective Against Disease?" also sheds some light on this aspect of the diabetes problem. The report on the experiment of the British physicians in using high-fiber diets on volunteers appeared in the July 24, 1976, issue of *Lancet*, while the University of Kentucky study appeared in the November 1979 *American Journal of Clinical Nutrition*. And reports on the work of Drs. Douglass and Rasgan have appeared in *Annals of Internal Medicine* (January 1975) and *Lancet* (December 11, 1976).

Dr. Shroeder's work on chromium is contained in his previously cited book *Trace Elements and Man*. Other books which offer further evidence of chromium's function in diabetes control are *Trace Elements in Human and Animal Nutrition* by E. J. Underwood, M.D. (New York: Academic Press, 1977) and *Zinc and Other Micro-Nutrients* by Carl C. Pfeiffer, M.D. (New Canaan, Ct.: Keats, 1978). For the study concerning chromium in the hair of diabetic children, see *Breakthroughs* by Charles Panati (Boston: Houghton Mifflin, 1980). And for Dr. Altshule's comment, see *Nutritional Factors in General Medicine*, cited earlier. As for periodicals see *Diabetes*, September 1977; the *Journal of Applied Nutri-*

tion, Vol. 30, No. 1 and No. 2, 1978; the *American Journal of Clinical Nutrition,* April 1977; and *Nutrition Reviews,* July 1968.

Garlic's ability to alleviate diabetes is detailed in Adams and Murray, *Health Foods, op. cit.,* while Dr. Lucidi's remarks are to be found in his earlier cited article in *Let's Live.* The *Australian and New Zealand Journal of Medicine* for December 1977 and the September 1978 *Journal of the American Podiatry Association* carry research reports on Vitamin B_6 and its need in the management of diabetes. The role of inositol, another B vitamin, in controlling diabetes is discussed in *Diabetes* (Vol. 26, Supp. 1, Abstract 154). In his previously cited book, Dr. Altshule notes that "some diabetics seem to utilize the B vitamins poorly and do well when receiving an oral B-complex preparation daily."

The landmark article on Vitamin C and diabetes appeared in *Perspectives in Biology and Medicine* (Winter 1974). It was written by George V. Mann, M.D., who pointed out, "Impairment of insulin junction function, whether by its absence, as in juvenile diabetes, or by its inhibition, as in adult-onset diabetes, will lead to impaired transport of vitamin C." The controversial Canadian cardiologist, Dr. Wilfred E. Shute, claims that Vitamin E is essential in the proper management of diabetes and describes some of his successes in using it to treat diabetes in his book *Vitamin E for Ailing and Healthy Hearts.* There is in any event little controversy regarding Vitamin E's capacity to improve circulation in the extremities, especially the legs, and circulation in the extremities is one of the most pronounced problems in advanced diabetes. For a round-up of research on Vitamin E and circulation, see the *New York Times,* September 30, 1973. The June 24, 1977, issue of *Science* contained a research report on Vitamin D and diabetes, while a Florida physician, B. F. Hart, M.D., wrote an interesting article in *Let's Live* (May 1978) regarding the potentially positive role of the bioflavonoids—

factors found with Vitamin C in its natural form—in controlling diabetes. For the study on exercise and diabetes, see the *New England Journal of Medicine,* November 29, 1979.

CHAPTER FIVE
LOW BLOOD SUGAR

The case of the Qoola Indians was first reported in *Science News,* February 3, 1973. Much of the material on its incidence, as well as an excellent, brief discussion of what it is, can be found in Frank Murray's *Program Your Heart For Health, op. cit.* For a more complete description of the disease, see *Low Blood Sugar and You* by Carlton Fredericks, Ph.D., and Herman Goodman, M.D. (New York: Constellation International, 1969). *Time* magazine of April 7, 1980, carried an article entitled "The Fad Disease" which, as its title suggests, questioned the prevalence of this ailment. But another popular magazine, *Parade,* published in its August 14, 1979, issue an article entitled "Neurotic—or Is It Your Diet?" which treated this malady more seriously. The quotes from Hawkins, Dunn, and Abrahamson are in the *Parade* article; the Mayo clinic study is reported in the *Time* article. For more complete information see Dr. Abrahamson's book *Body, Mind and Sugar* (New York: Avon, 1977) or Dr. Dunn's report in *New Dynamics of Preventive Medicine,* Vol. 2, Symposia Specialists, 1974. On the negative side, see the February 5, 1973, issue of the *Journal of the American Medical Association.* Meanwhile, the *Saturday Review* of February 4, 1978, told of an accident involving a Boeing 747 which was caused by a hypoglycemic pilot who, so an official investigation showed, had not been maintaining an adequate blood sugar level through a regular, well-balanced food intake. Incidentally, one of the first to call attention to the problem was a doctor who developed hypoglycemia only to find that his colleagues for the most part could not even diagnose it, much less cure it. As the physician in question, Dr. Stephen Gyland, put in a letter to the July 18, 1953, *Journal of the American Medical Association*, "During three years of severe illness I was examined by fourteen specialists and three nationally known clinics before a diagnosis was made."

The quote from Dr. Rogers, as well as the one from Dr. Hungerford, are taken from "Sugar Neurosis" which appeared in *Prevention*, August 1979. An interesting periodical, put out by syndicated magazines under a variety of titles such as *Nature's Way* or *Today's Living* and made available in health-food stores throughout the nation, published an article in July 1980 on the use of nutrition in probation work in Cuyahoga Falls, Ohio. For more detailed and scholarly material on nutrition's potential role in rehabilitating criminals, see the May 1976 *Monthly Memorandum* of the International Association of Preventive Medicine and the *Journal of Orthomolecular Psychiatry*, Vol. 4, No. 3, 1975.

The most thorough study on sugar and its effect on human health is *Sweet and Dangerous* by John Judkin, M.D. (New York: Peter H. Wyden, 1972). Dr. Yudkin is a London research physician who has filled his books with the numerous discoveries that he and others have made on the subject, and for those of us with a sweet tooth, his data make very grim reading. Dr. Shroeder's previously cited book was also a source for some of the material on sugar. Studies showing reduced resistance resulting from sugar ingestion have been published in the *Journal of the California State Dental Association*, 32, No. 9, 1964; the *American Journal of Clinical Nutrition*, 26, No. 2, 1973; and *Dental Practice*, December 1976. The quote from *Essence* appeared in an article by Roz Dunn, "Sugar: Kicking the Habit," in the January 1978 issue.

CHAPTER SIX
SICKLE-CELL ANEMIA, IRON-DEFICIENCY ANEMIA, AND SYSTEMIC LUPUS ERYTHEMATOSUS

A major source for information on the general problems of sickle-cell anemia was Shirley Motte Linde's *Sickle Cell: A Complete Guide to Prevention and Treatment* (New York: Pavillion, 1972). Because it is now almost a decade old, it does not contain any material on the more recent and quite promising developments in this field, but it does supply a good deal of basic information. Other sources drawn upon for the introductory section on the subject were "The Facts about Sickle-Cell Anemia" by Sandra Gregg in the August 1980 *Essence;* a story in the December 3, 1971 *Medical World News;* and some material on the subject in Adelle Davis's *Let's Get Well, op. cit.*

The Columbia University research into Vitamin E and sickle-cell anemia was reported in the July 1965 issue of the *American Journal of Clinical Nutrition.* For more material on the Oakland experiment and Vitamin E, see *Prevention* for July 1979. The experiment concerning zinc and its possible use in combatting the illness is described in the *Encyclopedia of Natural Healing* by Mark Bricklin (Emmaus, Pa.: Rodale Press, 1976). The *Encyclopedia of Common Diseases,* put out by the same publisher, carries a report on the research by Rockefeller and Cornell Universities on cyanate. For further material on this intriguing and, possibly, highly important aspect of the subject, see Robert Huston's articles in the November 1973 and August 1974 issues of the *American Journal of Clinical Nutrition.* The quote from the Sloan-Kettering official is taken from Ralph W. Moss's startling book, *The Cancer Syndrome* (New York: Grove Press, 1980). And Jacklyn McDonald's article appeared in the August 1980 issue of *Essence.*

The HEW study on iron deficiencies in premenopausal American women was discussed in *Ob Gyn News,* April 15,

1974. The hypothesis published by Dr. Deas on corn starch consumption as a possible cause of anemia in black women was advanced in the *Medical Tribune* of February 2, 1977.

That only 10 percent of ingested iron is absorbed was noted by Drs. Bruce M. Camitta and David G. Nathan in an article they published in *Postgraduate Medicine,* February 1975. That Vitamin C can improve this absorption rate has been reported in many scientific journals. See *Minnesota Medicine,* February 1970; *American Journal of Clinical Nutrition,* April 1968; *Internal Medicine News,* November 1974. For material regarding the role of the B vitamins in anemia, see the report by Doctors Trowbridge and Netland in the *Journal of the Maine Medical Association,* December 1964; the piece by Dr. de Vries in *Medical News,* April 7, 1967; and the article by Dr. Herbert in the *Journal of Clinical Nutrition,* September 1968.

For documentation on how Vitamin E can affect anemia, see H. J. Marvin's report in the *American Journal of Clinical Nutrition,* 12,88 (1963) and *Nutrition Reviews,* 20,60 (1962).

Lay literature on SLE is quite limited, but *Ebony* published an informative article entitled "Lupus Erythematosus" in its April 1979 issue, while *Scientific American* published "Systemic Lupus Erythematosus," an article by David Koffler, in its July 1980 issue. Also see the booklet put out by the National Lupus Foundation of St. Louis, Missouri, which is cited in the text. The quotation from Drs. Ayres and Mihan is from their report in *Cutis,* January 1979.

CHAPTER SEVEN
TOWARD A HEALTHIER BLACK AMERICA

Medical World News of January 29, 1971, carried a report of Dr. Burkitt's remarks to a conference in San Diego on cancer earlier that month. In these remarks, the British physician outlined his findings regarding fiber, findings based on his experiences in Africa. On June 29, 1971, the *British Medical Journal* carried an article by Dr. Burkitt and another British physician on the same subject. Much material has been published on the subject since. One useful book for laypersons is *The Save-Your-Life-Diet* by David Ruben, M.D., which was published in 1976 and is now available in paperback from Ballantine Books.

The question of how much protein a person can comfortably metabolize (process in his or her system) remains a somewhat controversial issue in health circles. An informative and balanced review of the literature on the subject can be found in *Nutritional Factors in General Medicine* by Mark D. Altshule, M.D. (Springfield, Ill.: Charles C Thomas, 1978).

Although the quote from Carlton Fredericks comes from one of his magazine columns, his case against white flour can be found in more detailed and documented form in his books. See, for example, *Food Facts and Fallacies* (New York: Arco), which has gone through seven printings since it was published in 1965.

In recent years evidence has begun to accumulate concerning the dangers of diets high in polyunsaturated fats. The latest is a Swedish study which appeared in the June 1981 issue of the *Journal of the American Medical Association*. It showed that men with the lowest levels of fats in their blood, including cholesterol, had the highest death rates from cancer and alcohol. In an accompanying editorial, the *Journal* noted, "Vegetable oils in the diet have been shown to be more potent promoters of carcinogens in lab animal tests than animal fats." Dr. Williams's statement regarding the utility of butterfat appears in Chapter Five of his book *Nutrition Against Disease,* cited previously. I personally regard this work as the best book on nutrition, and possibly the best book on health, that has ever been written. On the tendency of egg eaters to suffer fewer heart attacks than non-egg eaters, see *Executive Health,* August 1980.

For a report on the blood-pressure-and-coffee study conducted at IBM, see *Executive Health,* February 1979. The possible role of very moderate drinking in protecting the heart was spotlighted at a conference sponsored by the American Heart Association in March 1979. A report in the *New York Times* of March 20, 1979, gives a fairly comprehensive account of the research revealed at the conference.

For data on the way mineral deficiencies in the soil can and will cause mineral deficiencies in the crops grown in such soil, see *Nutrition Reviews,* 34:316 (1976). What you will find is a statement by the Food and Nutrition Board designed to denigrate the claim by "food faddists" that chemical fertilizers can affect the quality of the crops for which they are used. But, in the process of repudiating the claim, the Board tacitly concedes it by admitting that such fertilizers can affect the mineral composition of the soil and thus indirectly lower the quality of its plants.

The value of walking was detailed in a study published in the November 16, 1979, issue of the *Journal of the American Medical Association.* As for exercise in general, Frank Murray provides what I consider the best and most balanced summary of its role in health that I have yet seen in Chapter 20 of his valuable book, *Program Your Heart for Health.* Also see his Chapter 19 if you still feel any compunction about consuming eggs. The book is available in paperback (New York: Larchmont, 1977).

A lot has been written in recent years about the benefits of breast feeding to both mother and child. One article which summarizes much of this material in readable form is "The Case for Mother's Milk," which appeared in the *New York Times Magazine* on July 8, 1979.

The figures on the drop in death rates when doctors go on strike are supplied by Robert S. Mendelsohn, M.D., in his fascinating book, *Confessions of a Medical Heretic* (New York: Warner Books, 1979). In this book Dr. Mendelsohn goes so far as to say that "the greatest danger to your health is the doctor who practices Modern Medicine." What makes such a sweeping statement all the more startling is the fact that Dr. Mendelsohn has achieved a degree of eminence in his profession. He is chairman of the Medical Licensing Committee for the State of Illinois and is also professor of medicine at the University of Illinois Medical School.

The data about drug side effects causing so many hospital admissions were given me by Dr. Mark Altshule of the Harvard School of Medicine. Apparently Dr. Altshule also shares much of Dr. Mendelsohn's distrust of what their colleagues are doing and accomplishing, for he told me in this interview that "modern medicine is based largely on superstition." The statements by Dr. Rimland and by Dr. Ghadimi are from "Orthohealing" by Belinda Dumont, and they appeared in the February 1980 issue of *Omni* magazine.

The survey which showed that food stamps have lowered the nutritional levels of those receiving them was written up and distributed by the *Chicago Daily News* news service. It appeared in the *Boston Globe* of May 6, 1975, and presumably in other newspapers that subscribe to this service. It has definitely not received the attention it deserves.

In assessing the effectiveness of the American "healthcare" system, keep in mind that we spent 4.5 percent of our gross national product on health care in 1950. In 1980 we spent nearly 10 percent of our GNP on health care. During this period, death rates declined slightly for all races, but also during this period tens of millions of Americans, especially middle-aged men in the high-risk group, gave up cigarette smoking. Without such a switch, the death rate would most likely have remained the same or, quite possibly, might have gone up. Surely, there must be a better way to provide health care for all Americans.

Appendix

Nutritional Tables

Food	Approximate Measure	Calories	Calcium (mg)	Potassium (mg)	Sodium (mg)
DAIRY PRODUCTS					
Cow's milk					
whole	1 quart	660	1,140	210	75
skim	1 quart	360	1,192	215	78
Buttermilk, cultured	1 cup	127	298	52	19
Evaporated milk, undiluted	1 cup	345	570	102	38
Fortified milk, or pep-up	6 cups	1,373	2,949	2,704	248
High-calorie pep-up	⅔ cup	155	333	300	27
Low-calorie pep-up	4½ cups	738	1,792	1,015	84
Low-calorie pep-up	⅞ cup	148	358	203	17
Powdered milk, whole	1 cup	515	968	200	72
skim, instant	1⅓ cups	290	1,040	210	75
skim, noninstant	⅔ cup	290	1,040	210	75
Goat's milk, fresh	1 cup	165	315	66	8
Malted milk (½ cup with ice cream)	2 cups	690	270	60	19

Cocoa	1 cup	235	280	50	19
Yogurt, of partially skim milk	1 cup	120	295	50	19
Milk pudding (cornstarch)	1 cup	275	290	48	21
Custard, baked	1 cup	285	278	100	60
Ice cream, commercial	1 cup	300	175	170	140
Ice milk, commercial	1 cup	275	290	54	58
Cream					
light or half-and-half	½ cup	170	130	95	55
heavy or whipping	½ cup	430	82	65	50
Cheese					
cottage, creamed	1 cup	240	207	170	625
cottage, uncreamed	1 cup	195	202	180	620
Cheddar or American	1" cube	70	133	30	180
Cheddar, grated	½ cup	226	435	90	540
cream	1 oz	105	18	25	180
processed cheese	1 oz	105	210	22	370
Roquefort-type	1 oz	105	122	22	284
Swiss	1 oz	105	270	25	225

Food	Approximate Measure	Calories	Calcium (mg)	Potassium (mg)	Sodium (mg)
DAIRY PRODUCTS *(cont'd.)*					
Eggs					
boiled, poached, or raw	2	150	54	129	112
Scrambled, omelet, or fried	2	220	60	140	338
Yolks only	2	120	48	33	9
OILS, FATS, AND SHORTENINGS					
Butter	1 Tbsp	100	3	4	120
Butter	½ cup or ¼ lb.	800	22	28	990
Hydrogenated cooking fat	½ cup	665	0	0	4
Lard	½ cup	992	0	t	t
Margarine, ¼ pound	½ cup	806	22	58	1,150
Margarine, 2 pats	1 Tbsp	100	3	9	144
Mayonnaise	1 Tbsp	110	2	3	85
Oils					
corn, soy, peanut, cottonseed	1 Tbsp	125	0	0	0
olive	1 Tbsp	125	0	0	0

safflower, sunflower seed, walnut	1 Tbsp	125	0	0	0
Salad dressing					
French	1 Tbsp	60	3	0	—
Thousand Island	1 Tbsp	75	2	—	—
Saltpork	2 oz	470	t	19	1,350

MEAT AND POULTRY, COOKED

Bacon, crisp, drained	2 slices	95	2	65	600
Beef					
chuck, pot roasted	3 oz	245	10	340	50
hamburger, commercial	3 oz	245	9	320	100
ground lean	3 oz	185	10	340	110
roast beef, oven cooked	3 oz	390	7	350	60
steak, as sirloin	3 oz	330	8	320	60
steak, lean, as round	3 oz	220	11	300	62
corned beef	3 oz	185	17	60	1,200
corned beef hash, canned	3 oz	120	20	180	540
dried or chipped	2 oz	115	10	190	30
pot pie, 4½" diameter	1 pie	460	20	318	620
stew, with vegetables	1 cup	185	30	500	75

MEAT AND POULTRY, COOKED (cont'd.)

Food	Approximate Measure	Calories	Calcium (mg)	Potassium (mg)	Sodium (mg)
Chicken					
broiled	3 oz	185	10	350	50
fried, breast or leg and thigh	3 oz	245	13	320	50
livers, fried	3 medium	140	16	160	51
roasted	3½ oz	290	10	280	58
Duck, domestic	3½ oz	370	9	285	74
Lamb					
chop, broiled	4 oz	480	10	275	75
leg, roasted	3 oz	314	9	270	70
shoulder, braised	3 oz	285	8	260	60
Pork					
ham, cured, pan boiled	3 oz	290	8	370	1,000
ham, as luncheon meat	2 oz	170	5	290	700
ham, canned, spiced	2 oz	165	5	280	800
chop, 1 thick	3½ oz	260	8	390	30
roast	3 oz	310	9	360	40

sausage, bulk	3½ oz	475	7	270	958
Turkey, roasted	3½ oz	265	23	320	60
Veal					
cutlet, broiled	3 oz	185	9	400	70
roast	3 oz	305	10	390	70

VARIETY MEATS

Brains, beef, calf, pork, sheep	3½ oz	125	10	219	125
Chili con carne					
with beans	1 cup	325	98	500	1,060
without beans	1 cup	510	14	520	1,000
Heart, braised	3 oz	160	14	190	90
Kidney, braised	3½ oz	230	18	320	250
Liver					
beef, sautéed with oil	3½ oz	230	8	380	184
calf, 1 large slice	3½ oz	261	13	453	118
lamb, 2 slices	3½ oz	260	16	330	85
pork, 2 slices	3½ oz	241	15	390	111

Food	Approximate Measure	Calories	Calcium (mg)	Potassium (mg)	Sodium (mg)
VARIETY MEATS (cont'd.)					
Sausage					
bologna, 2 slices	1/8″ x 4″	124	4	110	550
frankfurter, 2	3/4″ x 7″	246	6	215	1,100
liverwurst	2 oz	132	4	75	450
Sweetbreads, braised, calf	3½ oz	170	7	244	116
Tongue, beef	3 oz	205	7	240	90
FISH AND SEAFOODS					
Clams, steamed or canned	3 oz	87	74	230	170
Cod, broiled	3½ oz	170	30	400	110
Codfish cakes, fried	2 small	175	—	—	—
Crabmeat, cooked	3 oz	90	38	100	900
Fish sticks, breaded, fried	5	200	12	140	—
Flounder, baked	3½ oz	200	22	585	235
Haddock, fried	3 oz	135	11	510	56
Halibut, broiled	3½ oz	182	14	540	56

Herring, kippered	1 small	211	66	—	—
Lobster, steamed	½ avg	92	65	180	210
Mackerel, canned	3 oz	155	221	—	—
Oysters					
raw, 6 to 8 medium	½ cup	85	113	120	80
stew, made with milk	1 cup	200	269	310	940
Salmon, canned	3 oz	120	160	340	45
Sardines, canned	3 oz	180	367	540	480
Scallops, breaded, fried	3½ oz	194	110	470	265
Shad, baked	3 oz	170	20	350	75
Shrimp, steamed	3 oz	110	98	205	130
Swordfish, broiled	1 steak	180	20	780	51
Tuna, canned, drained	3 oz	170	7	240	700

VEGETABLES

Artichoke, globe	1 large	8 to 44	50	300	30
Asparagus, green	6 spears	18	18	130	3
Beans					
green snap	1 cup	25	45	204	2
lima, green	1 cup	140	44	320	2

Food	Approximate Measure	Calories	Calcium (mg)	Potassium (mg)	Sodium (mg)
VEGETABLES (cont'd.)					
lima, dry, cooked	1 cup	260	15	306	1
navy, baked with pork	¾ cup	250	112	420	960
red kidney, canned	1 cup	230	74	750	6
Bean sprouts, uncooked	1 cup	17	19	514	3
Beet greens, steamed	1 cup	27	118	332	76
Beetroots, boiled	1 cup	68	24	324	64
Broccoli, steamed	1 cup	45	190	405	15
Cabbage					
as coleslaw	1 cup	140	47	240	150
sauerkraut, canned	1 cup	32	54	210	915
steamed cabbage	1 cup	40	78	240	23
Carrots					
cooked, diced	1 cup	45	38	600	75
raw, grated	1 cup	45	43	410	51
strips, from raw	1 medium	20	20	205	25
Cauliflower, steamed	1 cup	30	26	220	11

Celery					
cooked, diced	1 cup	20	54	300	80
stalk, raw	1 large	5	20	130	30
Chard, steamed, leaves and stalks	1 cup	30	155	475	120
Collards, steamed leaves	1 cup	51	282	393	40
Corn					
steamed	1 ear	92	4	300	t
cooked or canned	1 cup	170	10	400	472
Cucumbers, 1/8" slice	6	6	5	80	3
Dandelion greens, steamed	1 cup	80	337	750	130
Eggplant, steamed	1 cup	30	17	390	2
Endive (escarole)	2 oz	10	45	215	9
Kale, steamed	1 cup	45	130	260	29
Kohlrabi, raw, sliced	1 cup	40	66	520	10
Lambs' quarters, steamed	1 cup	48	460	—	—
Lentils	1 cup	212	50	505	15
Lettuce					
loose leaf, green	1/2 head	14	35	260	9
iceberg	1/4 head	13	20	175	9

Food	Approximate Measure	Calories	Calcium (mg)	Potassium (mg)	Sodium (mg)
VEGETABLES (cont'd.)					
Mushrooms, cooked or canned	½ cup	12	8	180	400
Mustard greens, steamed	1 cup	30	308	510	68
Okra, diced, steamed	1½ cups	32	82	370	1
Onions					
mature, cooked	1 cup	80	67	315	14
Raw, green	6 small	22	65	115	2
Parsley, chopped, raw	2 Tbsp	2	14	80	1
Parsnips, steamed	1 cup	95	88	570	11
Peas					
green, canned	1 cup	68	25	96	270
fresh, steamed	1 cup	70	22	200	1
frozen, heated	1 cup	68	19	135	115
split, cooked	½ cup	115	11	296	13
with carrots, frozen, heated	1 cup	53	25	160	84
Peppers					
pimientos, canned	1 pod	10	9	50	t

raw green, sweet	1 large	15	11	170	t
stuffed with beef and crumbs	2 medium	255	60	387	420
Potatoes					
baked	2 medium	100	13	500	4
french fried	10 pieces	155	9	510	6
mashed with milk and butter	1 cup	230	45	654	660
pan fried	¾ cup	268	15	775	225
scalloped with cheese	¾ cup	145	127	310	450
steamed before peeling	1 medium	80	11	407	3
chips	10	110	6	210	200
Radishes, raw	5 small	10	5	130	4
Rutabagas, diced	½ cup	32	40	170	4
Soybeans, unseasoned	1 cup	260	150	1,080	4
Spinach, steamed	1 cup	26	124	470	74
Squash					
summer	1 cup	35	8	480	8
winter, mashed	1 cup	95	23	510	2
Sweet potatoes					
baked	1 medium	155	36	300	12
candied	1 medium	235	50	360	18

Food	Approximate Measure	Calories	Calcium (mg)	Potassium (mg)	Sodium (mg)
VEGETABLES *(cont'd.)*					
Tomatoes					
canned, whole	1 cup	50	27	552	18
raw, 2" x 2½"	1 medium	30	16	360	5
juice, canned	1 cup	50	17	540	36
catsup	1 Tbsp	15	2	160	260
Turnip greens, steamed	1 cup	45	375	—	—
Watercress, leaves and stems, raw	1 cup	40	75	140	25
FRUITS					
Apple juice, fresh or canned	1 cup	125	15	200	5
Apple vinegar	½ cup	14	6	100	1
Apples					
raw	1 medium	70	8	130	1
stewed or canned	1 cup	100	10	210	4
Apricots					
canned in syrup	1 cup	110	28	600	2
dried, uncooked	½ cup	110	50	780	19

fresh	3 medium	55	18	280	1
nectar or juice	1 cup	140	22	440	t
Avocado	½ large	185	11	600	4
Banana	1 medium	85	8	390	1
Blackberries, fresh	1 cup	85	46	220	t
Blueberries, canned	1 cup	245	100	200	2
Cantaloupe	½ medium	40	33	910	40
Cherries					
canned, pitted	1 cup	100	37	135	8
fresh, raw	1 cup	65	18	270	1
Cranberry sauce, sweetened	1 cup	530	34	150	3
Dates, dried	1 cup	505	105	1,300	1
Figs					
dried, large, 2" x 1"	2	110	80	390	15
fresh, raw	3 medium	90	35	110	1
stewed or canned, with syrup	3	130	36	105	1
Fruit cocktail, canned	1 cup	195	23	350	12
Grapefruit					
canned sections	1 cup	170	32	237	2

Food	Approximate Measure	Calories	Calcium (mg)	Potassium (mg)	Sodium (mg)
FRUITS (cont'd.)					
fresh, 5" diameter	½	50	21	290	4
juice	1 cup	100	20	280	2
Grapes					
American, as Concord	1 cup	70	13	110	5
European, as Muscat, Tokay	1 cup	100	18	240	6
juice, bottled	1 cup	160	28	450	1
Lemon juice, fresh	½ cup	30	8	80	4
Lemonade concentrate, frozen	6-oz can	430	9	170	5
Limeade concentrate, frozen	6-oz can	405	11	118	t
Olives					
green, canned, large	10	72	65	45	1,400
ripe, canned, large	10	105	56	23	650
Oranges					
fresh, 3" diameter	1 medium	60	50	300	t
juice, fresh, 1 glass	8 oz	112	27	500	2
juice, frozen, concentrate	6-oz can	330	69	1,315	4

Papaya, fresh	½ medium	75	40	470	6
Peaches					
canned, sliced	1 cup	100	11	310	6
fresh, raw	1 medium	35	9	31	5
Pears					
canned, sweetened	1 cup	195	13	75	12
raw, 3" x 2½"	1 medium	100	13	182	3
Persimmons, Japanese	1 medium	75	7	310	1
Pineapple					
canned, sliced	1 large	95	26	150	1
crushed	1 cup	205	75	140	2
raw, diced	1 cup	75	22	210	1
juice, canned	1 cup	110	37	370	2
Plums					
canned in syrup	1 cup	185	20	213	2
raw, 2" diameter	1	30	10	100	t
Prunes, cooked	1 cup	300	60	810	10
Prune juice, canned	1 cup	170	34	625	5
Raisins, dried	½ cup	230	50	575	19

Food	Approximate Measure	Calories	Calcium (mg)	Potassium (mg)	Sodium (mg)
FRUITS *(cont'd.)*					
Raspberries					
frozen	½ cup	100	12	95	t
raw, red	½ cup	57	40	190	t
Rhubarb, cooked, sweetened	1 cup	385	112	510	15
Strawberries					
frozen	1 cup	242	50	220	3
raw	1 cup	43	20	157	2
Tangerines, fresh	1 medium	40	33	110	2
Watermelon, 4" x 8"	1 wedge	110	63	600	2
BREADS, CEREALS, GRAINS, AND GRAIN PRODUCTS					
Biscuits, 2½" diameter	1	130	61	40	208
Bran flakes	1 cup	117	25	480	960
Bread					
cracked-wheat	1 slice	60	16	50	125
rye	1 slice	55	17	52	120
white, 20 slices	1 lb loaf	1,225	318	720	2,655

Food	Measure				
whole-wheat	1 lb loaf	1,100	449	820	2,880
whole-wheat	1 slice	55	23	40	144
Corn bread of wholeground meal	1 serving	100	60	75	314
Cornflakes	1 cup	110	6	40	165
Corn grits, refined, cooked	1 cup	120	2	200	2
Corn meal, yellow	1 cup	360	6	284	1
Crackers					
graham	2 medium	55	3	45	90
soda 2½″ square	2	45	2	12	110
Farina	1 cup	105	31	20	33
Flour					
soy, full fat	1 cup	460	218	1,826	1
wheat, all purpose	1 cup	400	18	86	1
whole-wheat	1 cup	390	49	445	3
Macaroni					
cooked	1 cup	155	11	276	1
baked with cheese	1 cup	475	394	132	1,192
Muffins, of refined flour	1	135	74	62	211
Noodles	1 cup	200	16	—	—

BREADS, CEREALS, GRAINS, AND GRAIN PRODUCTS (cont'd.)

Food	Approximate Measure	Calories	Calcium (mg)	Potassium (mg)	Sodium (mg)
Oatmeal, or rolled oats	1 cup	150	21	142	508
Pancakes					
buckwheat, 4" diameter	4	192	249	245	464
wheat, refined flour, 4" diameter	4	250	158	135	470
Pizza, cheese, ⅛ of 14" diameter	1 section	180	157	96	525
Popcorn, with oil and salt	2 cups	152	4	—	646
Puffed rice	1 cup	55	2	57	t
Puffed wheat, presweetened	1 cup	105	4	110	180
Rice					
brown	1 cup	748	78	310	18
converted	1 cup	677	53	300	6
white	1 cup	692	46	247	4
flakes	1 cup	115	9	60	329
polish	½ cup	132	35	357	5
Rolls					
breakfast, sweet	1 large	411	42	56	185

Food	Measure				
refined flour	1	115	28	34	202
whole-wheat	1	102	46	100	225
Spaghetti					
with meat sauce	1 cup	285	25	670	1,017
with tomatoes and cheese	1 cup	210	45	407	955
Spanish rice with meat	1 cup	217	35	577	790
Shredded wheat, biscuit	1	100	13	116	1
Waffles, 1/2" x 4 1/2" x 5 1/2"	1	240	124	114	317
Wheat germ	1 cup	245	57	550	5
cereal, toasted	1 cup	260	32	530	1
Wheat-meal cereal, unrefined	1/4 cup	103	15	126	1
Wheat, unground, cooked	1/4 cup	275	40	174	1
SOUPS, CANNED AND DILUTED					
Bean soups	1 cup	190	95	445	1,007
Beef and vegetable	1 cup	100	12	165	1,067
Bouillon, broth, consommé	1 cup	24	2	129	780
Chicken or turkey	1 cup	75	20	—	751
Clam chowder, without milk	1 cup	85	36	225	1,099
Cream (asparagus, celery, etc.)	1 cup	200	217	295	1,058

Food	Approximate Measure	Calories	Calcium (mg)	Potassium (mg)	Sodium (mg)
SOUPS, CANNED AND DILUTED (cont'd.)					
Noodle, rice, barley	1 cup	115	82	69	1,224
Split-pea	1 cup	147	31	275	959
Tomato, diluted with milk	1 cup	175	167	417	1,055
Vegetable (vegetarian)	1 cup	80	32	170	855
DESSERTS AND SWEETS					
Apple betty	1 serving	150	14	100	151
Bread pudding with raisins	¼ cup	374	218	430	400
Cakes					
angelfood	1 slice	110	2	40	113
chocolate cake, fudge icing	1 slice	420	118	184	282
cupcake with icing	1	160	58	72	150
fruit cake, 2″ x 2″ x ½″	1 slice	109	29	165	52
gingerbread, 2″ cube	1 piece	180	63	111	119
plain cake, without icing	1 slice	180	85	40	150
sponge cake, without icing	1 slice	115	11	32	70

Candy					
caramels	5	104	40	48	55
chocolate creams	2	130	18	30	63
fudge plain, 1" square	2 pieces	370	13	132	180
hard candies	1 oz	90	0	0	8
marshmallows, large	5	98	0	2	13
milk chocolate	2-oz bar	290	72	192	47
Chocolate syrup	2 Tbsp	80	0	120	20
Doughnuts, cake type	1	135	23	26	80
Gelatin, made with water	1 cup	155	0	0	111
Honey, strained	2 Tbsp	220	2	22	1
Ice cream, custard (see Dairy Products)					
Ices, lime, orange, etc.	1 cup	117	t	t	t
Jams, marmalades, preserves	1 Tbsp	55	14	19	3
Jellies	1 Tbsp	50	13	15	3
Molasses					
blackstrap	1 Tbsp	45	116	585	19
cane, refined	1 Tbsp	50	30	185	3

DESSERTS AND SWEETS (cont'd.)

Food	Approximate Measure	Calories	Calcium (mg)	Potassium (mg)	Sodium (mg)
Pie, 9″ diameter					
apple	1 slice	330	9	106	400
cherry	1 slice	340	14	140	405
custard	1 slice	265	162	182	382
lemon meringue	1 slice	300	24	66	337
mince	1 slice	340	22	236	600
pumpkin	1 slice	265	70	219	285
Sugar					
beet or cane	1 cup	770	0	0	0
white, refined	1 Tbsp	50	0	0	0
brown, firm-packed, dark	1 cup	815	167	688	60
Syrup					
maple	2 Tbsp	100	41	70	4
table blends	2 Tbsp	110	2	10	1
Tapioca cream pudding	1 cup	335	262	337	390

NUTS, NUT PRODUCTS, AND SEEDS

Almonds				
dried	½ cup	425	163	541	2
roasted and salted	½ cup	529	163	541	140
Brazil nuts, unsalted	½ cup	457	124	476	1
Cashews, unsalted	½ cup	392	29	325	40
Coconut, shredded, sweetened	½ cup	174	8	176	0
Peanut butter				
commercial	½ cup	300	29	309	300
natural	½ cup	284	30	337	2
Peanuts, roasted	½ cup	190	37	337	2
Pecans, raw, halves	½ cup	343	36	300	t
Sesame seeds, dry	½ cup	280	580	360	30
Sunflower seeds	½ cup	280	60	460	15
Walnuts, English, raw	½ cup	325	50	125	1

BEVERAGES

Alcohol				
beer (4% alcohol)	2 cups	228	10	50	14
gin, rum, vodka, whiskey (86 proof)	1 oz	70	0	t	t

Food	Approximate Measure	Calories	Calcium (mg)	Potassium (mg)	Sodium (mg)
BEVERAGES *(cont'd.)*					
wines, dessert [18.8% alcohol]	½ cup	164	4	37	2
table wine [12.2% alcohol]	½ cup	100	10	100	6
Carbonated drinks					
artificially sweetened	12 oz	0	0	—	—
club soda	12 oz	0	0	—	—
cola drinks, sweetened	12 oz	137	0	—	—
fruit-flavored soda	12 oz	161	0	—	—
ginger ale	12 oz	105	0	—	—
root beer	12 oz	140	0	—	—
Coffee, black, unsweetened	1 cup	3	9	40	2
Tea, clear, unsweetened	1 cup	4	t	58	t
SUPPLEMENTARY FOODS					
Bone meal or powder	½ tsp	0	1,000	t	t
Calcium gluconate	7½ tsp	—	1,000	0	0
Calcium lactate	3½ tsp	—	1,000	0	0
Dicalcium phosphate	1 tsp	0	1,000	0	0

Desiccated liver, defatted	¼ cup	120	10	480	140
Lecithin, granular	2 Tbsp	105	t	t	t
Powdered yeast, brewer's					
debittered	¼ cup	91	70	631	40
primary, grown on molasses	¼ cup	115	81	600	165
torula	¼ cup	148	90	800	6
torula, calcium fortified	¼ cup	148	600	800	6

Source: U.S. Dept. of Agriculture

Index